E PUB IS ALWAYS BLATHERIN' ON ABOUT ● THE B
IE WAS JARRED AT A HOOL ● THE FECKIN' BOO
S EYES ● THE BOOK OF LUV ● E
E FECKIN' BOOK OF IRISH S OU
D FECKIN' BOOK OF IRISH S A H
RYTHING IRISH THAT'LL HAVE YE EFFIN' AN' BLIN
N' OUT BALLADS WHILE SCUTTERED, COOKIN' AN II
ME ARSE.' ● THE FECKIN' BOOK OF IRISH HISTORY
IE LAST 30,000 YEARS ● WHAT ARE WE FECKIN' L
N' IRISH SLANG THAT'S GREAT CRAIC FOR CUTE HO
S SOME SMART FECKER IN THE PUB IS ALWAYS BL
FELLA ALWAYS SANG WHEN HE WAS JARRED AT A I
NOT FIT FOR DACENT PEOPLE'S EYES ● THE BOOI
WERE A LITTLE GURRIER ● THE FECKIN' BOOK OF II
OWER OF SAVAGES ● THE 2ND FECKIN' BOOK OF II
● THE FECKIN' BOOK OF EVERYTHING IRISH THA
I' DEADLY QUOTATIONS, BELTIN' OUT BALLADS WI
AYING THINGS LIKE 'I WILL IN ME ARSE.' ● THE FEC
:N PAYING ATTENTION FOR THE LAST 30,000 YEAI
ACTERS ● THE BOOK OF FECKIN' IRISH SLANG TH
BOOK OF DEADLY IRISH QUOTATIONS SOME SM
● THE BOOK OF IRISH SONGS YER OUL' FELLA ALW
N' BOOK OF IRISH SEX & LOVE THAT'S NOT FIT FOF
:IPES YER MA USETA MAKE WHEN YOU WERE A LIT
HEN YOU GO ON THE BATTER WITH A SHOWER OF
AKES A HOLY SHOW OF THE FIRST ONE ● THE FEC

The Feckin' book
of Irish History
for anyone who hasn't been paying attention for the last 30,000 years

The Feckin' book
_of_ **Irish History**
for anyone who hasn't been paying attention for the last 30,000 years

Colin Murphy & Donal O'Dea

THE O'BRIEN PRESS
DUBLIN

First published 2009 by The O'Brien Press Ltd
12 Terenure Road East, Rathgar, Dublin 6, Ireland.
Tel: +353 1 4923333; Fax: +353 1 4922777
E-mail: books@obrien.ie
Website: www.obrien.ie

ISBN: 978-1-84717-069-9

British Library Cataloguing-in-Publication Data
Murphy,Colin
Feckin' history of Ireland. - (The feckin' series)
1. Ireland - History - Miscellanea 2. Ireland - History - Humor
I. Title II. O'Dea, Donal
941.5'00207

1 2 3 4 5 6 7 8 9 10
09 10 11 12

Cover design: Colin Murphy/Donal O'Dea
Printed and bound in the UK by CPI Mackays, Chatham ME5 8TD

'Ireland, sir, for good or evil, is like no other place under heaven, and no man can touch its sod or breathe its air without becoming better or worse.'

George Bernard Shaw,
Irish Playwright, 1856-1950

The Ice Age
How it feels during a typical Irish summer

🌿 During this period Ireland was joined to Britain by a land bridge to Scotland and it was from this general direction that a vast sheet of ice spread southwards and eventually covered most of the country. When the ice finally began to melt, sea levels rose by over 50 metres, making Ireland an island again, thanks be to Jaysus. As vegetation took hold, Ireland became home to many blood-thirsty, scavenging creatures, like wild bears, hyenas and many others. You can see examples of these creatures In Dublin's Kildare Street. And after you've seen them in the Dáil you can spend a little time viewing the stuffed versions next door in the Natural History Museum.

AFTER THE ICE MELTED CAME THE TIME OF THE MUCK SAVAGE.

Prehistoric Times

Before our land bridge to Scotland sank, stone age people had legged it across and started farming the land. There was no European Union to pay them for doing nothing at the time, so they quickly dumped that idea and started using their stone axes to kill and sacrifice each other. Evidence of their axes and many

WHY COULDN'T YOU BE HAPPY WITH A HEADSTONE
LIKE EVERYONE ELSE?

other weapons have been found in Limerick, which explains a lot when you think about it. It was during this period (about 3000 BC) that the amazing New-grange passage tomb was built, in which the small central chamber is illuminated by sunlight at dawn on the winter solstice – when there isn't a downpour out-side – an event which only happens approximately every 1,000 years!

Bogmen

In recent years the well-preserved bodies of two men were discovered in an Irish bog. They'd been sacrificed during prehistoric times. But the most fascinating discovery was that one had perfectly manicured nails and the other wore a type of hair gel made from vegetable oil. This, presumably, was intended to increase his attractiveness to girls. Sadly, all it attracted was an axe into the poor gobshite's skull.

WONDER WHO THEY'LL SACRIFICE NEXT

2000 – 500 BC

The Bronze Age

🌿 This was when the Celtic peoples first set foot in Ireland through Gaul and Britain, though it may surprise many to know that they weren't wearing green-hooped soccer shirts with 'Nakemura' written across the back. Because the soccer season hadn't started, they took up mining, found copper and tin, and – *Zut*

Alors! – or whatever they say in French – had bronze. These Celts were a very musical lot – Ireland boasts almost half the bronze-age musical instruments in the world, mainly horns and bells, on which they gave a stirring rendition of 'The Fields of Athenry'. This was also the time when Ireland's dolmen tombs were constructed, comprising three upright stones supporting a giant capstone weighing up to 100 tons. Most of the construction was done by Polish labourers as the Irish lot were down the road doing a nixer.

YEAH YEAH GUYS VERY FUNNY. HAR HAR.

La Tène Culture

These Celtic visitors originated in the La Tène civilisation in Switzerland. Disappointed that the Macgillycuddy Reeks didn't have much snow, not to mention ski lifts, they occupied themselves creating elaborate interwoven art and interlacing knotwork in jewellery, stone and manuscripts. Mercifully, no

NICE SWORD. LA TÈNE DESIGN ISN'T IT?

YEAH, BUT I FIND THAT BITS OF BRAIN KEEP GETTING STUCK IN THE ELABORATELY INTERWOVEN PATTERNS

cuckoo clocks! La Tène culture was virtually wiped out in Europe by the Romans, but when word spread around the Forum about the wojus traffic on Ireland's M50, not to mention the desperate health service, they decided not to invade us and so Ireland was one of the few places La Tène art continued, surviving the centuries to influence later masterpieces such as the Book of Kells as well as a bit of graffiti on a chipper in Cork which reads 'Keane for Taoiseach'.

The Book of Kells

(c. AD800, on display in Trinity College, Dublin) is one of the great masterpieces of western art and possibly the most valuable book in the world. It is a copy of the four Gospels in Latin and is renowned for its extraordinary array of illustrations and interlaced shapes. It was made from the skins of about 200 cows and the ink was a mixture of apple juice and soot! By the time they were finished, the monks were pretty sick of steak and apple pie.

The Kingdoms of Ireland

Ireland at this time was divided into 150 tiny little kingdoms, so it must have been a bitch for paparazzi to keep tabs on the shenanigans of all the royal families. Minor kings were subjects of a less minor king who in turn took his orders from one of the five provincial kings, the provinces being Leinster, Ulster, Connaught, Munster and Meath, in which was located the seat of the High Kingship of Tara. Among the more famous kings who ruled here were Niall of the Nine Hostages (AD 377-405.) More recently the area has been under the rule of Dick of the Fifteen Dossers (AD 2002-2007), who decided to build a giant motorway through one of the most important archaelogical sites in Ireland.

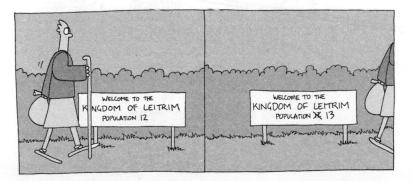

'St. Patrick... one of the few saints whose feast day presents the opportunity to get determinedly whacked and make a fool of oneself, all under the guise of acting Irish.'

— Charles M Madigan, American Journalist

AD 432

Arrival of St Patrick
The first real Paddy

In those days, the Irish regularly made wild plundering forays into Britain, much the way Irish Manchester United fans do most weekends. On one of these raids, they captured a youth of sixteen and kept him in slavery for six years. But the future St Paddy escaped, fled home, became a bishop, had a dream of converting us Pagan scum to Christianity, came back and did just that. Legend has it that he used the shamrock as a symbol to explain the Holy

Trinity and that he banished the snakes from Ireland, though a number still survive, disguised as county councillors. St Patrick's success in converting countless

FAIR PLAY TO YA PADDY!

fragmented, pagan kingdoms to Christianity is celebrated each year on 17 March by Irish and pretendy Irish people all over the world wearing giant styrofoam pastiches of him on their heads, drinking twelve pints of green beer, then puking into their chicken curry.

AD 500 – 800

Ireland's Golden Age

During this period Irish monastic settlements were considered the Harvard or Yale of their day, the key difference being that all the students didn't have yellow sweaters with tho sleeves tied across their shoulders and drive Porsches. Irish monks preserved much of Europe's written heritage and also set about re-Christianising the continent, missionaries forming churches as far away as Vienna and Kiev.

READ THIS AND YOU WILL FIND ENLIGHTENMENT

Peig

15

Among the most famous missionaries was Columcille, who converted the Picts of Scotland. Ireland became known as 'The Land of Saints and Scholars', as opposed to now when it's become known as 'The Land of Overpriced Apartments and Mindless Planning'.

INTERESTING STUFF

Thousand-year-old Dubs

In 1988 Dublin celebrated its 'Millennium', it being officially one thousand years old. There were several reasons this date was chosen. Firstly, in 988 the High King, Mael Sechnaill Mac Domnaill, deposed the Norse King of Dublin and renamed it Baile Átha Cliath, the Town of the Hurdle Ford. [Dublin was the original Norse name, from Dubh Linn meaning 'black pool'.] Of course any of a hundred other events could have been selected as the moment Dublin was founded. So another reason 1988 was picked was that the Eighties were really crap in Ireland economically and we needed to get more tourists to visit us. And finally it made a nice ryhming slogan: 'Dublin's great in '88.'

The Viking Invasions

Ruthless, cut-throat, driven by greed. But enough about Irish solicitors. Long before them came the Vikings, bent on raping and pillaging Ireland's fair land. Great sailors and fearsome warriors, they ploughed across the seas from Norway and Denmark in search of plunder, and found plenty. The unfortunate monks would be slaving away over precious gold chalices and the like, when in would burst a hairy Viking and bag the lot. Eventually the monks copped

Round Tower in Glendalough, County Wicklow

themselves on and built a load of tall round towers, from which they could look down on the invaders and yell 'Naa naa na-na-na'. After having their arses kicked a few times by the locals, many Vikings eventually decided Irish women were fine bits of stuff and started to marry them. They also founded Ireland's capital, Dublin, for which Cork people will never forgive them.

'The Irish forgive their great men when they are safely buried.'

— *Irish Proverb*

1014, Good Friday

The Battle of Clontarf
The Life (and Death) of Brian

Most Irish people think this great battle was about the legendary Brian Boru, High King of Ireland, heroically defeating the invading shower of Viking savages. In fact, it was mainly a row with the King of

Leinster, Mael Morda, who had the hump, not surprisingly, because Brian kept attacking him. So he formed an alliance with Sitric, the Viking King of Dublin, as well as Sigurd of the Orkneys and Brodir of the Isle of Man, all of whom planned to kill each other after the battle and take power. Lovely people. Anyway, it was all in vain, as the great Brian led his army to a heroic victory in Clontarf on Good Friday. Unfortunately, while he was back in his tent searching for his Easter eggs, the fleeing Brodir attacked and killed him. In typical fashion, Irish people have commemorated Brian Boru not with a giant monument but by naming a pub after him. In Glasnevin. 4 km from Clontarf.

INTERESTING STUFF

Up to this time it was commonplace for Irish priests and monks to have girlfriends, get married and have noisy little chislers bawling all over the monastery. Then Pope Gregory introduced celibacy and spoiled all the fun. From then on, the only bad habits they were allowed were the ganky ones they wore.

NOTE TO ENGLISH READERS:

It was at this point in Irish history that England began to involve herself in our affairs. Granted, the English were invited here by an Irishman. But you know how it is when you ask your friends around for dinner and they're still sitting there yapping away at three in the morning and won't leave until you throw them out. Unfortunately the situation in Ireland was a little similar, the key difference being that it didn't take a few hours to get rid of our English friends, but almost eight centuries! During that time, as you may be aware, your ancestors did a few nasty things to the Irish and it's unavoidable mentioning them. In fact, given the nature of this book, it's pretty unavoidable slagging the hell out of the Englishmen and women who repeatedly did the dirty on us. And there is a *lot* of slagging, because you unfortunately gave us a lot of material to work with! Think of it as payback for all those pathetic Irish jokes we've had to put up with over the years! Anyway, that's all in the past now and Ireland and England are great friends. Especially since you gave us Jack Charlton.

21

The Arrival of the Normans

Not to mention the Nigels, Reginalds, Basils, Ruperts and Cecils.

Brian Boru's death left Ireland's leadership pretty banjaxed and various wannabe high kings vied for power. The last native High King of Ireland was Rory O'Connor, who came to power in 1166 and set in motion a chain of events that would result in Irish people forever after cheering for England's opposition in every sport from soccer to tiddlywinks. Rory insisted on persecuting the King of Leinster, Dermot MacMurrough, who was so cheesed off he barrelled across to England to ask King Henry II for help. Henry hooked him up with the Earl of Pembroke, who had the deadly nickname of Strongbow, and before you could say 'I'll have a pint of cider and a packet of crisps', Dermot was back in Ireland with a moxy load of Norman soldiers. Before long they'd captured Wexford, Waterford and Dublin. Dermot was stuck with them now, as were the rest of us for the best part of a millennium. Wouldn't you just love to go back in time and give Dermot a good root up the arse for bringing all those centuries of misery on our heads?

1171

henry II in Ireland

King Henry started to panic that Strongbow was getting a little too big for his boots in Ireland and might end up actually establishing a rival kingdom over here, so now he himself hopped aboard a ship and, in 1171, became the first English King to set foot on Irish soil, his first step going directly into fresh cowshit (wishful thinking).

Henry immediately made his son, John, the 'Lord of Ireland' and when Henry kicked the bucket a few years later and John became king, this 'lordship' shite meant that Ireland was now ruled directly by the English Crown. By the way, Strongbow made up with Henry and eventually got control of Leinster again. You can visit him in Dublin's Christ Church Cathedral. Well, not so much him as his tomb. He probably wouldn't be much of a conversationalist after 850 years.

1177

The Invasion of Ulster
The English start to put the boot in

The first serious English influence in Ulster came when John de Courcy, who had arrived in Ireland with Henry II, decided to launch an invasion of eastern Ulster. Despite heavy resistance and several attempts on his life (mainly by cholesterol poisoning through feeding him the Ulster Fry breakfast seven days a week), de Courcy established bases at Newry, Carlingford, Coleraine and Downpatrick. English control of Ireland was now spreading slowly across the entire island, the bowsies.

JUST A LIGHT SNACK BEFORE THE FIGHT, MR DE COURCY

The Pale

Around this time the only people in Ireland who gave a fiddler's feck what the King of England had to say were those living in an area on the east coast which included what is now Dublin, Meath, Louth and a bit of Kildare. The boundary of these lands was called 'The Pale' and anyone living outside this was considered by the arrogant inhabitants as a bit of a savage, hence the expression 'Beyond the Pale'. Nowadays, The Pale refers to the white patches on your arse after you've been sunbathing on the Costa Blanca.

1150 – 1300

The Normans in Ireland

Although they originally came to kick the living shite out of us, over the next century or so the Normans and their descendants gradually came to fancy some of the local talent and many a roll in the heather was had by a big hairy Norman and an even hairier cailín.

In fact, the Normans even began to speak Gaelic and adopt our laws and centuries-old customs, like bribing councillors and ripping off foreigners.

You can still see the influence of the Normans on Ireland in the many stone castles and churches scattered around Ireland

MR AND MRS NORMAN AND THEIR SON OISÍN

which date from the 12th-13th century, like Trim Castle or St Patrick's Cathedral in Dublin. Ireland's public transport system also dates from this era.

1315 – 1318

Edward Bruce King of Ireland

Any enemy of England is our bosom buddy

In 1314, the Scots, led by Robert Bruce, crushed the English at the Battle of Bannockburn. Naturally delighted with this turn of events and with the hopes of doing a bit of English-crushing themselves, chieftains in northern Ireland invited Robert's wily brother Edward to take the Irish crown. Edward accepted and in 1315 landed in Ireland with 6,000 Scots, 8,000 sets of bagpipes, 20,000 haggises and an accent that sounded like he'd been educated in Uzbekistan. (The bagpipes and haggises are idle speculation). He quickly captured Carrick-fergus Castle, which became his base, and in 1316 he was crowned King of Ireland at Dundalk. The next year, keen to make life a real pain in the arse for the English, big brother Robert arrived with reinforcements and this Irish Scots alliance roamed the country with a considerable degree of suc-cess, enjoying victories in the west and south. However they failed to take Dublin, and eventually Edward was killed in battle at Faughart in County Louth in 1318, ending the uprising. His last words were reputedly, 'Ach yeeeel ochdenay en de denny gloch', which not even his own brother could understand. Maybe it had something to do with the axe sticking out of his chest?

ARGH!! I GIVE UP!

'The English are not happy unless
they are miserable, the Irish are not
at peace unless they are at war, and
the Scots are not at home unless
they are abroad.'

George Orwell, English Novelist, 1903-1950

1366

The Statutes of Kilkenny

No sex with the Irish please, we're British

Throughout the 14th century the Normans and native Irish had more and more begun to share their language and customs, not to mention their beds. The new King of England, Edward III, decided enough was enough. He didn't want his subjects mixing with a bunch of illiterate, smelly, back-stabbing scum – and the Irish were his subjects, after all. And so a meeting of Parliament, convened in Kilkenny, enacted a set of laws designed to stop the Normans becoming 'more Irish than the Irish themselves'. These included banning Normans from speaking Irish, dressing like the Irish, going bareback on their horses, inter-marrying, mixing with Irish musicians and poets or playing hurling, particularly as the Irish kept hammering them 7 goals and 25 points to 0 goals and 3 points.

Unfortunately for Edward, the Normans were already so Irish that, in true Irish fashion, they completely ignored his stupid bleedin' laws.

1394 – 1399

King Richard II in Ireland

Richard II would make two trips to Ireland in his lifetime (and become the last English King to visit for over 300 years, thank Christ). His first trip in 1394 was for a stag weekend with the lads in Dublin's Temple Bar, during which he also managed to repulse the King of Leinster, Art MacMurrough, and force the public submission of most of the other Gaelic leaders, who, due to England's preoccupation with wars elsewhere, had been winning back territory. (Richard also had a domestic problem: his French wife was only seven years of age and it was really embarrassing when, in the middle of a royal feast, your wife kept saying that she had to go have a 'do-do'.) Richard had no sooner plonked his arse back on his throne in England than MacMurrough attacked again. Now really pissed off, Richard returned to take on the King of Leinster again in 1399. But MacMurrough had learned from his previous defeat and pretty much sent Richard packing with his royal sceptre between his legs. He died in prison in England a year later.

'The Irish are a fair people. They never speak well of one another.'

———— *Samuel Johnson, English Poet and Writer. 1709-1784*

The Black Death 1348-55

Like most of Ireland's troubles, the Black Death spread to Ireland from England, carried over by rats on English ships trading with Dublin and Drogheda. And while fatalities were minor compared with the rest of Europe, where 40-50 million died, it did have a devastating effect on many communities. However, survivors finding that a neighbour's entire family had bitten the dust, simply took over their land and belongings. Every cloud has a silver lining.

1315 – 1500

The Great Earls of Ireland

The King gives us all a slice of our own cake

The English found it most annoying that we Irish kept killing English soldiers every time they tried to kill us. I mean, really, the nerve of us. So to placate us, the

English monarchy created three Earldoms in Ireland. One branch of the Fitzgerald family was given the Earldom of Kildare, another Fitzgerald branch was given the Earldom of Desmond and the Butler family were given the Earldom of Ormonde. By the next century, these three controlled almost all of southern Ireland, with the exception of the Dublin region, where English rule still prevailed, (and Dubliners were starting to say things like 'Allo, 'allo, 'allo. Cor blimey, Guvnor!') In contrast to the situation in the south, north of the border the two historically powerful families of the O'Neills and the O'Donnells were batin' the shite out of each other on an almost permanent basis. What is it about the north of Ireland? Is there something in the water or wha'?

SORRY, CHAPS, YOU SEEM TO BE MISSING THE POINT HERE. WE DO THE KILLING, AND YOU DO THE DYING?!??

32

Poynings' Law
The law that outlaws law-making

Although it sounds like one of those formulae you had to learn off in chemistry class, i.e. $X + Y(EM) = C$, where Y is the co-efficient of water, in fact, Poynings' Law was actually the English monarchy's latest formula for making Ireland obedient. Sir Edward Poynings arrived in Drogheda in 1494 at the behest of Henry VII to summon the Irish parliament in order to inform them that they could no longer summon parliament. At least, not without the English parliament's permission. Neither could they pass any laws. Any laws passed in England would now also apply in Ireland. This unfortunate state of affairs would endure for three hundred years. And to this day, the passing of urgent legislation in the Dáil seems to take the same length of time.

Henry VIII's influence

If you think we had it bad under English rule up to now, well, things were about to become seriously worse. When the Pope wouldn't grant him a divorce from Catherine of Aragon on the grounds that she couldn't give him a male heir (not to mention that she had a face like a bag of spanners), Catholic Henry split from the Church in Rome and declared

Ye olde English custom of rubbing opponent's nose in it...
Rarely practised these days

himself head of the English Church. He began a process of brutally enforcing English customs, dress and language across Ireland, and, by Jaysus, the way the English dressed in those days was particularly brutal. Among the deeds carried out on old Henry's behalf was the supression of a rebellion by Silken

Thomas, son of the Lord of Kildare, (who Henry had despatched to the Tower of London). When Thomas's garrison had surrendered, everyone was executed, with the exception of Silken Thomas's infant half-brother. Ahh, they were so nice. Melt your heart, wouldn't it?

'Other people have a nationality. The Irish and the Jews have a psychosis.'

———— Brendan Behan, Irish Playwright, 1923 - 1964

1531

The Repression of Catholicism

After breaking from Rome, Henry VIII realised this was the ideal opportunity to get more lands and money for himself and his cronies. Allegiance to Rome meant treachery to the crown, so all over England he simply had church lands removed from the Catholic bishops' possession, not to mention having many a bishop's head removed from his possession. He also began this process in Ireland, and, while he got his hands on lots of land, the ordinary people weren't exactly queuing down the street to convert to Protestantism. Seems they'd heard disturbing rumours about how abstemious, strict and utterly dull Protestantism was, and that while it was bad enough that Catholic mass went on for two hours, a Protestant service could last up to four!

In 1541 Henry was officially declared King of Ireland, and by now his policy of planting Protestants in Ireland, stealing the locals' land and then renting it back to them had taken a firm hold in the psyche of English crown, and would endure throughout the reign of many a subsequent monarch. Happily, Henry himself would only endure a handful of years more, and kicked the bucket in 1547. And not a bleedin' moment too soon.

How the Tories got their name

Many of today's British Conservative Party might be disturbed to know that their nickname, 'Tories', originated in Ireland in the mid-sixteenth century, deriving from the Gaelic word 'toraidhe', which meant plunderer, robber, thief, barbarian and general yobbo. Even though they officially changed their name to 'Conservative', the original name seems to have stuck. I wonder why?

1553 – 1558

Queen 'Bloody' Mary

At last, a Catholic Queen in England. Thanks be to Jaysus. Finally a bit of relief for the Irish. You must be joking! The daughter of Henry VIII, Mary was determined to return England to Catholicism. Deeply religious (it's always a worry when you hear that), Mary proceeded to achieve her goal, not through prayer, dialogue or diplomacy, but by having all her dissenters burnt at the stake. Lovely woman. Over in Ireland, attacks on the Pale were continuing, so she decided to extend her influence to an area immediately outside the Pale, ie counties Offaly and Laois. This she did by removing

the current owners (mainly the O'Connors and O'Moores) and replacing them with English settlers. Naturally, the dispossessed were a little bit miffed about this and started attacking the bastards who'd stolen their land. But in true extremist religious fashion, Mary had a solution for this, too. She invited the O'Moores and O'Connors to a peace conference. And then had them all brutally slaughtered. Which crime, if there is any basis to Bloody Mary's religious beliefs, must mean that she's now adorning the sharp end of one of the prongs of Satan's trident while being held over a roaring fire.

Queen Elizabeth I

The Virgin Queen as she was known, (but not in the Biblical sense, where she wasn't known at all) may have been one of England's greatest monarchs, but the Irish didn't think much of her. Having restored Protestantism to England, she then tried to impose it on Ireland and quickly discovered, like her predecessors did, that if us Irish are going to sin, we're going to sin in our own religion, thank you very much. Which resulted in Elizabeth's reign being marked by three great rebellions – those of Shane O'Neill (1559), the Fitzgeralds of Desmond (1568–83), and Hugh O'Neill (Tyrone) and Hugh O'Donnell (Donegal) (1594–1603). The US state of Virginia was reputedly named after Elizabeth's supposed virginity. The town of Fukyu in China is also named after her.

I LOST MY VIRGINITY LAST NIGHT

REALLY? I'VE LOST MINE 12 TIMES ALREADY.

Shane O'Neill

Shane O'Neill was one of the most colourful characters in Irish history, the main colour being blood red. Often described as brutal, uneducated and savage, Shane quickly realised he'd do well in politics. During his career he killed his brother and nephew, battled his father, accumulated vast wealth and lands and kept his mistress chained in a cellar until such time as he fancied a quick roll in the sack.

However, he was a brilliant soldier and led his men from the front, defeating all the local chieftains and the English on three separate occasions. He was eventually murdered after he got rat-arsed at a banquet. A fitting end.

1595 – 1603

The Nine Years' War

Hugh O'Neill, Earl of Tyrone, having allied himself with Red Hugh O'Donnell of Donegal, scored major successes in 1595, defeating Queen Elizabeth's forces at Clontibret and capturing Blackwater Fort. In 1598 he knocked the stuffing out of another English force at the Battle of Yellow Ford near Armagh. Enraged at this upstart repeatedly kicking the crap out of her bigger, much better equipped armies, Elizabeth then sent the largest ever expeditionary force (20,000 men) to Ireland, under the command of the 2nd Earl of Essex, to subdue the rebels. But Essex basically made a hames of it, wandering around the south engaging in skirmishes, slowly having his men picked off and watching his army dwindle until he was forced to make a truce with O'Neill. Back in England, Lizzie, who'd had a romantic relationship with Essex, was so embarrassed by this she was forced to cut off all ties with the Earl, not to mention everything else from his neck up.

Red Hugh O'Donnell Escapes Dublin Castle

At the tender age of fifteen, the British got Red Hugh O'Donnell plastered drunk and took him hostage, holding him and his friends, Art and Shane O'Neill, in Dublin Castle for four years. Then, in January 1592, he led the others in a famous escape that basically involved getting through a drain in the jacks floor which emptied into the Poddle River, which was essentially a sewer. Talk about going through the motions! And if that didn't stink enough, Art broke his leg climbing over a wall and the others had to carry him – forty miles over the snow-covered Wicklow mountains. Sadly, Art didn't make it and Hugh lost both big toes to frostbite. But they remain the only three people ever to escape from Dublin Castle.

1601

The Battle of Kinsale

Nowadays, Kinsale in County Cork is a picturesque harbour village with a reputation as one of the gourmet centres of Ireland. In 1601, however, it's quite likely you'd have found dogs/cats and anything else on four legs on the menu, as the town had been under siege from Elizabeth's 12,000-strong army under Lord Mountjoy for three months. Inside the walled town were 4,800 Spanish soldiers sent by King Philip of Spain, because he was so narked at the British destruction of his famed Spanish Armada two years earlier. Unfortunately for us, the Spanish didn't actually take part in the battle, due to misunderstandings and miscommunication, ie they spoke Spanish and we spoke Irish, so when told to 'Ionsaí ag breacadh an lae' (attack at dawn) the Spanish leader, Aguila, thought the Irish wanted a recipe for paella. Meanwhile, Hugh O'Neill had been forced to march his army the length of Ireland from his power base in Ulster in the depths of winter in order to confront Mountjoy. His men arrived weak and hungry. Worse, his allies, Red Hugh O'Donnell and Richard Tyrell, had failed to arrive by the agreed time. On Christmas Eve, 1601, Mountjoy left some of his forces to guard the town and attacked O'Neill's army with artillery and cavalry. As a result, most of the Irish soldiers woke on Christmas morning to find that Santa had left them a large, sword-shaped hole in their chests. At that point O'Donnell decided that a holiday in the sun was long overdue and escaped with the surviving Spaniards. O'Neill fled back to Ulster and surrendered two years later, two days after Elizabeth died, so she never knew her policies of repression in Ireland had, for the foreseeable future, succeeded. Ha Ha.

The Aftermath of the Spanish Armada

After their defeat by the British (September 1588) in the famous sea battle, the Spanish Armada tried to leg it around the west coast of Ireland, but were hit by a terrible storm. As many as 5,000 men died when their ships were driven against the razor-like rocks. Most drowned but many made it ashore, only to be hunted down by the British. A handful, probably less than 100, survived and blended into the local communities, a neat trick considering they spoke only Spanish and looked like they'd been on a sunbed for six hours. Legend has it that they interbred with the local cailíns, and you can still recognise their descendants today in villages on the west coast – they're the ones singing 'Y Viva España' when they're pissed.

'A man who is not afraid of the sea will soon be drowned... for he will go out on a day he shouldn't. But we do be afraid of the sea, and we only be drownded now and again.'

—John Millington Synge, Irish Playwright & Poet, 1971-1909
(from 'The Aran Islands')

The Flight of the Earls

The great significance of the battle of Kinsale was that it marked the beginning of the end of the old Gaelic order which had survived since ancient times. Over the coming centuries Ireland's way of life would increasingly feel the influence of British culture (fish & chips, lager louts, Spice Girls etc). In 1607 the Earl of Tyrconnell, Rory O'Donnell (brother of Red Hugh), had all but given up on reversing the situation, and, along with about 100 other chieftains, decided to get the hell out of Ulster before the axe fell, literally. Hugh O'Neill meanwhile had been summoned to London, and, making a calculated guess that it wasn't for tea and scones with the king, decided to join Rory on the ship, which landed in the Netherlands. This became known as 'The Flight of the Earls' and it sowed the seeds

of the conflict in Ulster centuries later. Hugh O'Neill died in exile in Rome in 1616, apparently from boredom at being constantly surrounded by priests.

The Plantation of Ulster

England plants a boot into Catholic Backsides

With the Irish leaderless, the English crown decided to solve the 'Irish problem' once and for all by simply kicking them off their land, giving it to Protestants settlers and dumping the locals in the poorest areas of the province, all in the true spirit of Christian kindness for which the head of the English church (the King) was famed. The finest land was divided into plots, usually over 1,000 acres, and granted to 'undertakers' – not the guys who stick you in a coffin, but men who undertook to run these huge estates and settle them with people of English and Scottish extraction. To the Irish, though, they were in effect nailing the lid on their way of life and their rights. While this mostly worked in Ulster, their attempts to convert the greater population of the country to Protestantism were as successful as a one-legged man in an arse-kicking contest.

47

Derry/Londonderry - what's in a name?

In 1613 James 1 gave Derry to the London Companies (a bunch of stockholders who were given other people's lands to colonise) as a 'gift'. It's not every day you get a whole city as a pressie. They promptly changed the city's name to Londonderry. The nationalists have always ignored this, and signs in the South continue to point to 'Derry' while signs in the unionist-dominated North point to 'Londonderry'. Which essentially means tourists can get lost. A local compromise is 'Stroke City'.

1641

The Rebellion of 1641
We try to uproot some planters

Civil war was looming in England, which was great, as for once they'd be slaughtering each other instead of us. Charles 1 was in conflict with his parliament and basically needed eyes in the back of his head to see what we were up to. Perhaps sensing that Charles soon wouldn't even have a head, a certain Sir Phelim O'Neill decided to take advantage of the situation to wrest control of the country from the English/Protestant settlers. O'Neill was a member of a minor branch of the famous Hugh O'Neill clan, who had retained some power and title as a reward for siding with the English in the Nine Years' war. He was a lawyer who'd been trained in London and was well integrated into planter society. However, he believed that English repression and forced seizures of lands had gone too far. Taking advantage of his planter background, he used the pretext of a dinner invitation from another leading planter, Sir Toby Caulfield, to seize the suckor's fort at Charlemont and launch the revolt. The rebellion was to be on two fronts – Dublin and Ulster. The Dublin one failed due to an informer, but in Ulster it was initially a resounding success. Unfortunately, after the early military triumphs, the native Catholics, bent on revenge, massacred at least 12,000 Protestants and left thousands more homeless, thereby proving that they could be just as big a bunch of bastards as their oppressors.

Ireland Unites

With the English Civil War under way, English forces in Ireland found themselves badly stretched and they mostly retreated to their strongholds and garrison towns like Drogheda (and being stuck in Drogheda is something you wouldn't wish on your worst enemy). This left effective control of the country to the leaders of the 1641 rebellion and their supporters, who included the entire Catholic population, the Old English (descendants of the original Norman settlers who had long since gone native) and the contemporary Anglo-Irish settlers – everyone the English had pissed off, in fact, which was about 95% of the country. The Irish decided to better organise the popular uprising they'd initiated, and met in 1642 to form the Confederation of Kilkenny, which was essentially an Irish government.

JOLLY BAD FORM HAVING AN UPRISING WHILE WE'RE BUSY KILLING EACH OTHER, DON'T YOU THINK?

JUST... NOT...CRICKET...

The Confederation of Kilkenny

The King's ok, as long as he's Catholic

The ambitions of the Confederation were to secure full rights for Catholics and self-government for Ireland. They also swore allegiance to Charles 1 (talk about backing the wrong horse). The motto of the Confederation was *Pro Deo, Rege et Patria, Hibernia Unanimis* (which, loosely translated, meant: 'Come on ye boys in groon' and 'Up the King'). Their royal allegiance was due to the fact that the English Parliament had threatened to invade Ireland and destroy the Catholic religion and Irish land-owning class, which,

BLESSED IS HE WHO DISMEMBERS AND KILLS THOSE OF OTHER FAITHS, FOR THINE IS THE KINGDOM OF HEAVEN ...

not surprisingly, left them feeling just a teensy weensy bit uneasy. The newly-formed government immediately set about raising taxes (don't they always) to fund their war effort and sent envoys to sympathetic regimes in Europe. Pope Innocent X was among those who actually chipped in with a load of arms and money, keen no doubt to impress Jesus by helping to dismember as many Protestants as possible, irrespective of the fact that they believed in the same Jesus. Jaysus!

INTERESTING STUFF

Kilkenny Castle – sold to the man in the Restoration jacket!

The venue for the Catholic Confederation was Kilkenny Castle, one of Ireland's most beautiful ancient buildings. Parts of the castle were built around 1200. In the 1960s the building was sold to the local restoration group for £50, which was pretty good value considering a one-bed apartment in Kilkenny would later cost about 10,000 time that amount!

The Battle of Benburb

News of the Confederation also brought about the return of many Irishmen exiled in Europe. Among these was Eoghan Roe O'Neill, who had valuable experience of disembowelling Dutch Protestants, against whom he'd successfully campaigned for the Spanish. O'Neill's aims were: complete independence, Ireland restored to Roman Catholicism, overturning of the plantation of Ulster and the restoration of his clan's ancestral lands in Ulster. Nobody could accuse him of lacking ambition! He also happened to be a bit of a genius when it came to military strategy and used it to great effect when a bunch of Scots Presbyterians decided to invade Ireland to get revenge for the earlier massacres of Protestants and also to convert Ireland to a Presbyterian state, as if we didn't have enough bleedin' religious wars here already. The Scots army under Munro numbered 6,000 and was equipped with cannons. O'Neill's numbered 5,000 and had no cannons. Yet O'Neill's clever strategy forced the Scots back into the bend in a river, trapping them there. When the battle was over, Munro had lost 5,700 men to O'Neill's 2,500. In other words, a serious arse-kicking.

'If one could only teach the English how to talk, and the Irish how to listen, society here would be quite civilised.'

—— Oscar Wilde, Irish Playwright, Poet and Novelist, 1854-1900

1649

Oliver Cromwell

Eoghan Roe O'Neill died in 1649, which was unfortunate as Cromwell also invaded that year and we could have really done with a decent military strategist to deal with the brutality that was to come. Charles 1's head was adorning a spike somewhere and the English Parliament had decided that their greatest threat now lay in the opposition of English royalists in Ireland as well as the Catholic Confederation. So along came Cromwell with a 20,000 strong army. He attacked Drogheda, and when the town surrendered, slaughtered the 3,500 survivors, including the women and children. He did the same in Wexford, as well as burning most of the town. He went on to take Kilkenny, Carlow and Clonmel. One of the olden phrases coined to recall his presence in Ireland goes: 'What a low-life murderous scum-sucking gouger of a shitehawk'. He pissed off back to England in 1650 and tried to justify his genocidal campaign several times in his later life, which of course was impossible. He died in 1658. All together now, 'Hip Hip ...'

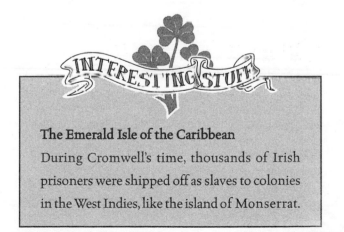

The Emerald Isle of the Caribbean

During Cromwell's time, thousands of Irish prisoners were shipped off as slaves to colonies in the West Indies, like the island of Monserrat.

In 1637 a group of Irish Catholic pilgrims had fled persecution in nearby St Kitts and also settled on the tiny tropical paradise. The rest of the population was made up of African slaves and a minority of English colonists. Naturally, the Irish got it together with the Africans, and today the locals sound like an Ethiopian guy who's been living in Cork for ten years! It's also the only country outside Ireland to officially celebrate St Patrick's Day!

1649 – 1661

To Hell or to Connaught
Early Attempts at Decentralisation

Cromwell's successors in Ireland continued their master's work with relish. They banned all public practice of Catholicism and hunted down priests and executed them (which saved the locals from having to listen to hour-long sermons). They confiscated all Catholic-owned property as well as lands owned by anyone who was in any way seen as anti-Cromwellian, which, considering what a murderous bollix he'd been, was pretty much everyone. They also transported approx 12,000 men, women and children as slaves to the West Indies, where at least they wouldn't have to put up with the crap Irish summers. Those who'd been booted off their land were offered a choice: accept a tiny lump of lousy, utterly useless rocky land in the west of Ireland or take this sword through your guts. Which gave rise to the expression of the day, 'To hell or to Connaught'. When the monarchy was restored in England in 1660 with a new king, Charles II, Irish Catholics were given faint hope of some justice. But Charles had other things on his mind – he managed to father at least twelve illegitimate little beggars by different mistresses in his time. He also, bizarrely, had Cromwell's body exhumed and subjected to a posthumous execution. So, while clearly a little loopy, he can't have been all bad.

⬆ HEAVEN
⬆ PURGATORY
⬇ HELL
⬇ CONNAUGHT

The Martyrdom of St Oliver Plunkett

🌿 Oliver Plunkett had been ordained in 1654 at the Irish College in Rome and was subsequently appointed Primate of All Ireland by Pope Clement IX. He set about restoring the institutions of the Catholic Church in Ireland. (One of his first problems was not the English, surprisingly, but the fact that many of his priests were rat-arsed with drink half the time, having turned to alcohol for comfort during the hard times.) Initially successfully with his reforms, the Jesuit College he'd established in 1670 in Drogheda was levelled to the ground by, guess who, in 1673. He went into hiding, refused to renounce his religion and continued to minister to his flock in secret. He was eventually arrested in 1679 on trumped-up charges of having tried to organise an invasion of 20,000 Frenchmen (I mean, come on, who the hell would ever want to organise that?). Plunkett was a highly admired intellectual and a pacifist, and, recognising that he'd never be found guilty in Ireland, the English staged a kangaroo court in London, where he was sentenced to death for promoting the Catholic faith. His gruesome execution involved being hanged, disembowelled and quartered, thereby demonstrating the traditional restraint for which the Brits are famous the world over. He was canonized in 1975, having had several miracles attributed to him. Although repeated novenas have been made to him in recent times to get the government to sort out the Irish health service, it seems this miracle is beyond even his powers of intervention.

INTERESTING STUFF

Oliver Plunkett's Head

Even after his execution poor Ollie would still have a hard time of it. First of all his body was buried in two boxes, then dug up and moved to a monastery in Germany. His head was then separated from the rest of him and went on a little jaunt to Rome, then to Armagh and finally to Drogheda. Most of what was left of his body was then shifted to Bath in England but a few bits stayed in Germany! Plunkett's head eventually ended up preserved (and on display) in St Peter's Church in Drogheda. It's enough to do your head in.

HOW'S THE HEAD, OLLIE?

1689

The Apprentice Boys

Part of Northern Protestant lore, the Apprentice Boys are, to this day, a symbol of Protestant resistance to Irish Republicans in general and to Catholicism in particular. At this time another Catholic, James II, had assumed the throne in England, which really put the willies up Protestants everywhere, not to mention the English Parliament, who promptly replaced him with a nice, comforting Prod – William of Orange from the Netherlands. But James wasn't done yet (well actually he was, but just didn't know it). He landed in Ireland where he had substantial support, and sent his loyal deputy, Richard Talbot, north to seize the Protestant city of Derry. But just before they arrived, a bunch of thirteen apprentice boys dropped their spanners, hammers and screwdrivers, seized the keys to the city gate and slammed the doors shut in the face of James's army. A siege ensued which was the longest ever in Ireland or Britain, lasting 105 days – even longer than it feels like when watching a Liverpool match. It claimed the lives of 4,000 people, half the population of Derry. During the siege the inhabitants were forced to dine on dogs, cats and rats. It was relieved on 28 July when three ships loyal to William sailed up the River Foyle, broke through the barrier and restored  supplies to the city. Today, there is a plethora of US fast food outlets in Derry, so dining conditions haven't changed much.

King Billy outside Carrickfergus Castle.

'When I told the people of Northern Ireland that I was an atheist, a woman in the audience stood up and said, "Yes, but is it the Catholic God or Protestant God in whom you don't believe?"'

Quentin Crisp, English Writer, 1908-1999

1690

The Battle of the Boyne
King Billy walks on water

The battle was between the Protestant King William III and the deposed Catholic King James II, who happened to be William's father-in-law. (You wouldn't want to go to their gaff for a family dinner). Besides being an attempt by James to depose William, the battle had a much wider European dimension – basically many European countries were scared shitless that France under Louis XIV was planning to bid adieu to their freedom. So, because Louis' soldiers were fighting for James, you had a real mixed bag of Euro soldiers opposing William. King Billy's side were a mix of English, Irish, Scots, Danes, Dutch and French Protestants as well as Dutch Catholics (and this might horrify a few present-day Orangemen – King William actually had the backing of the Vatican!). James's lot were mainly Irish and French Catholics as well as some German Protestants. So it was a great way to

meet different nationalities and hack them up into little pieces. William out-thought and outnumbered James, crossed the Boyne in County Meath and kicked the crap out of James's army. William went on to be King of England while James made himself as scarce as shite from a rocking horse by legging it to France. King Billy's victory is celebrated by Orangemen in Northern Ireland on 12 July every year.

1690

The First Siege of Limerick

Limerick kicks ass!

With James gone, his army (the Jacobites) retreated in the main to Limerick, thereby giving the city its reputation for having lots of people carrying sharp weapons. Their leader was Patrick Sarsfield, a very able commander dedicated to Ireland and the rights of Catholics. William arrived at the walls of the city on 27 August, cock-a-hoop after his victory at the Boyne and with an army of 25,000 who were all keen to get back to the Netherlands, possibly because of the liberal drug laws. His problem was that his siege cannon were still en route, and, in a daring move, Sarsfield intercepted the supply train at Ballyneety and blew the bejaysus out of William's supplies. William attempted an attack nonetheless and lost 3,000 men. He lost another 2,000 to disease as the siege dragged into the winter. Having had enough of freezing his arse off beside the Shannon, he sensibly returned to the Netherlands. Besides the obvious legacy of having changed the direction of Irish history forever, his other great bequest to Ireland is that half the population of the North are called Billy.

Patrick Sarsfield

Although born in Lucan in west Dublin, Patrick Sarsfield is remembered as a hero of Limerick, first for his leadership during the siege of the city and also his daring raid on Cromwell's supply train at Ballyneety. In Limerick he has a bridge, a street and a barracks named after him. Forced to flee Ireland, he entered the French service and fought in Flanders. On 19 August 1693 he was struck down in battle, and, as he watched the blood flow from his mortal wound, said, 'If only this had been for Ireland.' If only we had a few leaders like you around nowadays, Paddy.

The Second Siege of Limerick

The new Williamite commander, Godert de Ginkell, (obviously the bad fairy won at his christening) took his lot north where he inflicted a further defeat on the Jacobites at the Battle of Aughrim. The survivors retreated to Limerick where the lads had been strengthening the defences all winter and spring. But over a period of months and with the help of heavy artillery, Ginkell succeeded in blowing a hole in the walls the size of a Government Minister's expense account. He then attacked the outer defences at Thomond Bridge, with a ferocity only equalled by the All Blacks at Thomond Park, and when the Irish retreated, the French merde-heads slammed the gates shut. The 600 Irish outside were massacred or drowned in the Shannon. Unsurprisingly, there was 'a

cooling in Franco-Hibernian relations' after that. Patrick Sarsfield realized that hope was fading, gave the French commander a boot up the derrière and, left with little alternative, began negotiations to surrender. Ginkell agreed to a Treaty which would ensure Limerick's civilian population were unharmed, tolerate the Catholic religion throughout Ireland, guarantee against the confiscation of Catholic-owned land and allow Sarsfield and the Jacobite army to be transported to France. Naturally, after Sarsfield and the army were gone, the terms were ignored.

The Wild Geese

Under the terms of the Treaty of Limerick, the English agreed to let 14,000 soldiers, along with 10,000 women and children, leave for Europe, where most would join foreign armies (mainly French, Spanish, Austrian, Italian, Swedish, Russian), form Irish Brigades, and end up fighting the English again. They were referred to as the Wild Geese. Others would distinguish themselves in different fields, such as politics, which explains the presence of so many cute hoors throughout the governments of the continent. And over the next 100 years, continued oppression by you-know-who would see almost half a million Irish flee to the continent, much like any bank holiday weekend nowadays.

THE WEEKEND WILL BE OVER BY THE TIME WE GET OUT OF THIS BLEEDIN' KIP.

The Penal Laws
It sort of becomes illegal to be Irish

The Wild Geese probably had the right idea, as the English were now determined to make things even worse for the Irish. Over the coming years they enacted a series of Penal Laws designed to leave the Catholic majority penniless, powerless and extremely pissed off. Under these laws, Catholics couldn't hold

BASICALLY, YOU CAN'T DO ANYTHING, SO JUST SIT THERE AND BE QUIET.

public office, marry a Protestant, own a firearm, get a foreign education, join the army, enter parliament, vote, become a lawyer or judge, build a church from stone, enter Trinity College, own a horse worth more than a fiver, adopt an orphan, educate their young, etc etc etc etc etc. Besides making the English Protestant settlers rich, these laws had one ultimate goal – to make Catholics' lives so miserable that they'd simply fade away, leaving one great big Protestant paradise. What they didn't realise was that Catholics bleedin' thrive on being miserable.

'When anyone asks me about the
Irish character, I say look at the
trees. Maimed, stark and misshapen,
but ferociously tenacious.'

——————————— *Edna O'Brien, Irish Novelist, b 1930*

Sean na Sagart: Priest Hunter

Being a Catholic priest was a dangerous occupation in those times, so they went about in disguise and held masses in secret, pursued by 'priest hunters' – former criminals who hunted priests for bounty. The most famous was Sean na Sagart from Mayo, who used to fake oncoming death so he could give his last confession – only to stab the poor eejit of a priest when he leaned close to the 'sinner'. Bounty on a priest was £20 – a small fortune in those days. Sean was reputedly killed by the pissed off brother of one of his priest victims – not surprisingly he never had the chance to give his last confession! He is buried in unconsecrated ground under a tree that has never blossomed!

1700 – 1800

Protestant Ascendancy

During the next century, Protestants gained ownership of roughly 95% of all the land in Ireland, despite the fact that 80% of the population was Catholic.

This was a golden age for the English Protestant aristocracy, who built palatial mansions on vast country estates for themselves while their tenant Catholic farmers were so hungry they would have licked food off a scabby leg. Famines in 1727-30 and 1740-41 added to Catholics' misery and tens of thousands died. London's agricultural policy also made it more economical to breed cattle rather than grow grain, which required less labour, so many of the already struggling tenant farmers were basically considered to be of less worth than a cow and were unceremoniously booted off the land and evicted from their homes. Still, it's better to be a cow than a complete pig.

SALE ON

FREE IRISHMAN
WITH EACH COW
PURCHASED

1750 – 1800

The Beginnings of Mass Emigration

In Ulster, discrimination against Catholics and, for that matter, Presbyterians, had reached such heights (or depths) in the early 18th century that many were simply giving up the ghost and getting the hell out of the place. So much so that in 1708 Belfast had a population of around 3,000, of whom Catholics numbered seven! Protestant tenant farmers were benefitting from the growing linen industry while Catholic farmers hadn't a shirt on their backs, linen or otherwise. Each year as many as 5,000 Catholics and Presbyterians were heading for the US. A significant proportion of them were, unknowingly, heading for the bottom of the Atlantic, as so many died on the three-month journey. The Irish were among the very first wave of settlers that would lay the foundations for the modern United States of America, and eventually teach future generations of Americans how to drink properly.

1760 – 1790

Secret Societies

As a direct response to the treatment of Catholics, particularly tenant farmers, a whole rake of illegal groups sprang up during the 18th century. These had colourful names like Whiteboys, Steelboys, Defenders or Levellers. They mostly spent their time hamstringing horses and cows, driving herds of cattle over cliffs, poisoning animal feed, clubbing other farm animals to death. Naturally, the Protestant landowners, not to mention the cows, resented this deeply. And when they began to intimidate the landowners and their agents, military force was used to stamp them out. Many were arrested and killed, and a local priest, Fr Nicholas Sheehy from County Cork, who'd spoken out against the treatment of farmers, was arrested for sedition and hanged, drawn and quartered. While considerably weakened, the various movements continued nonetheless throughout the century. In Ulster, meanwhile, the Catholics had slowly been starting to crawl their way back up the economic ladder. In response to this, Protestants formed their own secret society, the Peep-O-Day-Boys, who were just as good as the Whiteboys etc at hamstringing cows but absolutely brutal at picking a name for a secret society.

'Ireland, thou friend of my country in my country's most friendless days, much injured, much enduring land, accept this poor tribute from one who esteems thy worth, and mourns thy desolation.'

— *George Washington, 1732-1799, First President of the United States, regarding Ireland's support for America during the revolution.*

INTERESTING STUFF

Where Gulliver's Travels Began

The Dean of St Patrick's Cathedral in Dublin is most famous for his creation of *Gulliver's Travels* – not a children's story as many believe, but a brilliant satire on the politics and morals of his time. In one scene the giant Gulliver puts out a fire in the Lilliputian government palace by pissing on it! Oh, if only we had the chance, Kildare Street would be flooded! Swift also invented the term 'yahoo' – a vile, lazy and filthy creature. The love of Swift's life was Esther Johnson or 'Stella' as he called her, though they never married. Swift became a champion of Irish social causes in later life and when he died left his money to found St Patrick's Hospital for the mentally ill – which still exists.

'It was a bold man who ate the first oyster.'

Jonathan Swift, Irish Novelist,
Dean of St Patrick's Cathedral, 1667-1745

Grattan's Parliament
They let us make a few decisions on our own

The locals were revolting in the United States. But, hey, soap was expensive. They were also rebelling against the British, which was causing the Brits some concern. As were the French, with their Revolution and their snappy 'Liberty, Equality and Fraternity' slogan, which went totally against everything the Brits had always stood for in Ireland, where they'd been using the slogan 'Brutality, Discrimination and Kick their Catholic Arses' for centuries. The last thing they needed was war on another front, so they decided to cut the Catholics a break or two before Ireland exploded.

One of the main campaigners for Catholic rights was the Protestant MP, Henry Grattan. In the 1770s many of the original Penal Laws were repealed and in 1782, the Irish Parliament was granted independence from the English parliament, mainly as a result of Grattan's efforts. This would become popularly known as 'Grattan's Parliament'. Henry Grattan would later campaign in favour of complete Catholic emancipation and against the Act of Union.

The United Irishmen

Although some reforms had been achieved, many felt that things were moving far too slowly (we'd only had 600 years of oppression at this stage) and that the liberal members of the Protestant Ascendancy were in reality only being paid lip service by their English masters. One of these was Theobald Wolfe Tone, a Protestant, now considered the founding father of modern day Irish republicanism. Tone openly promoted a doctrine that was completely alien to the English, involving equality, justice, freedom and things like that. He believed in an Ireland free from sectarianism and also free from English people. His ideas appealed to northern Presbyterians and in 1791 he and his supporter, Thomas Russell, met in Belfast and the United Irishmen was officially formed. Modern day bigoted Catholic republicans don't like to mention the fact that their founding fathers were a

couple of Protestants and a bunch of Presbyterians.
Irony's great, isn't it?

1795

Wolfe Tone's Exile
French leave

Tone quickly established a branch of the United Irishmen in Dublin and started to put pressure on the government to implement reforms. Naturally, these were ignored. The United Irishmen began to consider other options, like blowing a few heads off. Tone sought help from the French. Unfortunately the agent he contacted turned out to be a large lump of merde – he was an informer. The Dublin branch of the United Irishmen was crushed and Tone had to flee to America. From there he went to France where he continued

AVEZ VOUS UN
TREZ GRAND BOMB
S'IL VOUS PLAIT?

his efforts to get the French to invade Ireland, thereby killing two birds with one stone – booting out the English and finally introducing some decent restaurants into the country.

1795

The Orange Order
No Catholics need apply

On 21 September 1795, a group of Catholic 'Defenders' (see Secret Societies) went to Winter's pub near Loughgall, County Armagh which they'd identified as a meeting place for the 'Peep-O-Day-Boys'. They intended to make it final closing time for their Protestant counterparts. But they hadn't counted on their opponents being so well armed, and in the skirmish thirty Defenders were given their last orders. Not a single Peep-O-Day-Boy fell. In the aftermath, hundreds of Catholic homes and many churches were burnt out. Afterwards, three of the Peep-O-Day-Boys leaders, Daniel Winter, James Wilson and James Sloan, met and changed the group's name to The Orange Order, in honour of William of

Orange (King Billy of the Boyne fame), and because they were tired of being slagged off about the other name. As a sectarian organisation, perhaps their greatest contribution to history has been to halt the decline in the sale of bowler hats.

FECKIN' QUOTES

'The Irish don't know what they want and are prepared to fight to the death to get it.'

—————— *Sydney Littlewood, English Lawyer, 1895-1967*

INTERESTING STUFF

Captain Bligh and the North Bull Wall

The North Bull Wall, a favourite place for a lover's stroll for Dubliners, was actually designed by Captain William Bligh in 1800, about ten years after the famous 'Mutiny on the Bounty' occurred!

The statue of Mary, Star of the Sea
on Dublin's North Bull Wall

The Rebellion of 1798

Some you win, some you lose.

The rebellion long planned by the United Irishmen finally took place over several months in the spring and summer of 1798. It got off to a bad start when all of the Dublin leaders were betrayed by an informer. In fact, not only did it have a bad start, but with a couple of minor exceptions, pretty much had a bad middle and a bad end as well. The rising went ahead in Kildare and Meath and was brutally suppressed by the British. In Ulster, the rebels under Mc-Cracken were crushed almost immediately. A force of about 1,000 rebels under General Joseph Holt did manage to hold out in the Wicklow mountains until the autumn, and in Wexford the rebels briefly took control of almost the entire county before the Brits

sent in 20,000 troops and all but wiped them out. Not content with defeating the rebels, the British often massacred surviving prisoners, and in Enniscorthy and New Ross actually burned survivors alive. In retribution, fleeing rebels burnt 100 loyalists alive in a barn in Scullabogue, thereby provoking more acts of brutality by the English. And so it goes round. And round. And round.

Lord Edward Fitzgerald

The Lord Edward Pub beside Dublin's Christ Church cathedral is named after one of the conspirators in the 1798 rebellion, Lord Edward Fitzgerald, who was eventually captured and killed in Dublin. In his earlier life he had served as a British officer in the American War of Independence (clearly before he saw the light), during which his life was save by a freed negro slave called Tony Small, who would remain Edward's companion until he died. On a visit to Ireland Tony met a fine Irish cailín in Kildare and they married. You can just imagine the stares Tony got in the local pub in those days! Lord Edward was also an officially adopted chief of the Huron tribe of North America. A brave man in every sense, then.

1798

The Death of Wolfe Tone

In 1796 Wolfe Tone had accompanied a French fleet carrying an invasion force of 15,000 soldiers into Bantry Bay, County Cork only to be prevented from landing due to persistent storms. Jammy bastards, the English. On 22 August 1798, another French force arrived in Killala Bay in Mayo, though this one only contained 1,000 soldiers. However, joined by about 5,000 locals, they inflicted a heavy defeat on the Brits at Castlebar, a battle which became known as The

Castlebar Races, in honour of the speed at which the British reputedly took to their heels (tut-tut). Unfortunately, the French/Irish were subsequently defeated in County Longford. The French were allowed to return home, the Irish survivors were massacred, naturally. A couple of weeks later, Wolfe Tone returned with another French force of 3,000 soldiers. They

were intercepted by a much larger force from the Royal Navy and, after a battle which lasted only a few hours, Tone was arrested before a single French soldier could set foot on dry land and breathe garlic into an Irish girl's face. Tone was sentenced to death and asked for execution by firing squad. This was refused, so he cut his own throat in prison and died a few days later. Nasty. 1798 became known in the West of Ireland as 'The Year of the French' due to all the Gallic participation in Ireland's failed rebellion and because they were fed up to the back teeth with 'The Year of the English', which seemed to have been going on for centuries ... oh, hang on, it *had* been going on for centuries.

INTERESTING STUFF

The Union Flag

Many Irish people will be horrified to realise that the Union Jack actually contains a red saltire (diagonal cross) known as St Patrick's Cross, representing Ireland. The flag design originated when the Act of Union officially made Ireland part of Britain. The other diagonal is the saltire of St Andrew, for Scotland, while the main red vertical is the cross of St George, for England. The Welsh don't have a cross on the flag, a fact of which they are immensely proud.

The Act of Union

A lousy act to follow

Despite its failure, the 1798 rebellion had seriously put the willies up the English, who were terrified that Ireland would be used by one of its enemies (now numbering pretty much everyone on the planet) as a back door to an invasion of England. So they cooked up the Act of Union, meaning the Irish Parliament would be abolished and Ireland would be ruled from Westminster. The first attempt to get the Irish Parliament to vote itself out of existence failed by five votes, thanks largely to Henry Grattan making some impassioned speeches. But what are speeches compared to good old bribery? All sorts of goodies were then offered to various Anglo-Irish MPs – honours, land, power and straightforward cash – if they'd vote for the Act. The bastards rolled over and the second time around the Act was passed by forty-three votes. Ireland had now officially become a part of Britain. Modern day Irish politicians drew a valuable lesson from this scandalous event – if you want something, simply bribe someone.

YES, NOW I SEE THE ERROR OF MY WAYS. IRELAND'S
INTERESTS ARE BEST SERVED BY HANDING POWER
BACK TO THE NICE PEOPLE ON THE MAINLAND

INTERESTING STUFF

Michael Dwyer
and guerilla warfare in Wicklow

Michael Dwyer was a United Irishman who retreated to the Wicklow Mountain after the failure of the 1798 rebellion and, along with
General Holt, conducted a guerilla warfare
campaign against the British. So successful
were they that the British had to commit thousands of troops, build new barracks and even a
road (the Old Military Road from Sally Gap in
the Dublin Mountains). Dwyer commanded

such loyalty that once, when completely surrounded in a house, a colleague deliberately drew British gunfire and died so his leader could escape. After fighting for six years, Dwyer surrendered, on the promise that he and his family could emigrate to America. True to form, the British instead sent him as a prisoner to Australia, where, ironically, he would eventually end up as a Police Chief!

'Ireland is a peculiar society in the sense that it was a nineteenth century society up to about 1970 and then it almost bypassed the twentieth century.'

——————— *John McGahern, Irish Novelist, 1934-2006*

The cottage Michael Dwyer escaped from
after the 1798 Rebellion

William Pitt and George III

William Pitt was the British Prime Minister who promoted the Act of Union. Unlike many of his predecessors, however, he actually had sense enough to realise that if he didn't start treating Irish Catholics with a teensy-weensy bit of justice, he'd soon be up to his nads in rebels again. Unfortunately, his support for Catholic rights was opposed by the monarchy (surprise, surprise) in the form of King George III. This is the guy who had been treated for madness but had now been declared well when, clearly, the old gobshite was still a few cans short of a six-pack. When the nutter refused to honour the promise of Catholic emancipation, Pitt resigned, to his credit. Westminster then proceeded to pass a series of laws giving the army and police in Ireland almost carte blanche to kick the crap out of the peasantry and anyone else who opposed them. Naturally, the new powers were used to the full.

Robert Emmet's Rebellion

Robert Emmet was one of the participants in the failed 1798 rebellion. A Protestant and the son of a respected surgeon, Emmet fled to Paris after the rising and spent a great deal of time asking Napoleon for a few francs to pay for anti-Brit devices, e.g. guns, knives, pikes, swords, bows, arrows, cleavers etc. Unfortunately, Shorty was as tight as a camel's arse in a sandstorm and Emmet returned to Ireland empty-

SERIOUSLY, ARE YOU READY TO DO BATTLE TO THE DEATH?

NAH. LETS GO TO THE PUB INSTEAD.

handed. However, he continued to plan a new rebellion and used his meagre family legacy to buy and manufacture arms. Saturday 23 July 1803 arrived and unfortunately so did too many rebels from Kildare – Emmet had nowhere near enough weapons for them. Also he'd decided to keep his plans secret in case of informers, so secret in fact that most of the potential rebels thought the whole shebang had been called off and either went home or to the nearest pub. In the end the number of 'rebels' was reduced to a mob of about 100 whose main act of rebellion was to pull the Lord Chief Justice of Ireland, Lord Kilwarden, from his carriage and hack him to death. Realising that everything had gone pear-shaped, Emmet called the rebellion off. He escaped and hid in Rathfarnham for a time, but because he wanted to bo near his true love, Sarah Curran, he moved his hiding place to Harold's Cross and a few days later was captured (why couldn't she have gone to him in Rathfarnham?). He was tried and sentenced to be hanged and beheaded. Twenty-six other rebels were also executed. Emmet made a famous speech from the dock which included the often-quoted line: 'When my country takes her place among the nations of the earth, then and not till then, let my epitaph be written.'

Anne Devlin

One of the unsung heroines of Irish history, Anne was Robert Emmet's housekeeper in Rathfarnham, County Dublin. After the rebellion she was captured and tortured mercilessly but never gave a single name to the British. They even forced her to watch Emmett's execution. She was brutally treated for years before being released in 1806. She died in desperate poverty in the Liberties in 1851. In recent years a statue of Anne has been erected at the entrance to Rathfarnham village.

1814

The Apprentice Boys Mark II

Formed in 1814 and inspired by the actions of the Derry Apprentice Boys who slammed shut the gates of Derry on the approaching James II in 1689, the modern order of Apprentice Boys are anything but boys. In fact, the age profile of the present-day membership is such that many of them wouldn't have the strength to slam shut a garden gate. They were set up partially in response to the organised Catholic gangs such as the Defenders. In 1824 another similar organisation was formed, called the No Surrender Club. Subsequent organisations were called the No Fenian Bastards Brigade, the Burn the Scumbag Papist Brotherhood and the All Tagues Must Die Screaming Society. Like the bigotted Catholic republicans who hate the idea that their founding fathers were Protestant, it really gets on the tits of modern day Fenian-hating loyalists that the original Apprentice Boys all spoke Irish as their first language!

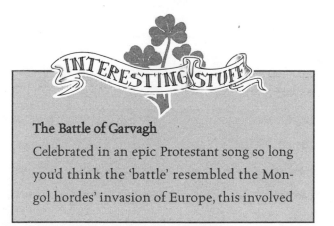

The Battle of Garvagh

Celebrated in an epic Protestant song so long you'd think the 'battle' resembled the Mongol hordes' invasion of Europe, this involved about 500-1,000 Catholic Ribbonmen (another Secret Society) armed with sticks, attacking a pub full of Protestants, who happened to have a few rifles with them. They shot three of the Ribbonmen and the 'battle' was over! A few Orangemen were found guilty of manslaughter but, thanks to a slightly biased jury, they got off scot-free, an act for which some of the jury got their names in the song: 'Mr Price and brave George Hill ... cleared the Boys of Garvagh'.

1800 –1830

Secret Rural Societies
Shhhhhh

In the era of the Napoleonic Wars, the mostly absentee Protestant landlords prospered by supplying Britain's armies with food. The landlords' tenants (poverty stricken Catholics, as well as many equally poor Presbyterians, who the British didn't care for either) had to hand over most of their crops just to pay the exorbitant rents. The same policies had given rise in a previous age to gangs such as the Defenders. Now came the likes of the Molly Maguires and The Ribbonmen. Same shit, different day. The Ribbonmen liked to attack and sometimes kill landlords, or in the event of their unavailability, their agents. They also liked to burn crops and property, preferably with somebody in it. Ribbonmen were basically anti-British, anti-Protestant, anti-landlord and pro independence. So, as you can imagine, the Ribbonmen and the Apprentice Boys got on like a house on fire. Literally.

(Regarding the Irish)

'This is one race of people for whom psychoanalysis is of no use whatsoever.'

Sigmund Freud, Austrian Psychiatrist, 1856-1939

1798 – 1810

Daniel O'Connell

Apart from making Donegal famous – no, that's Daniel O'Donnell – easy mistake – O'Connell has more main streets in Ireland named after him than any other person. Born in County Kerry, O'Connell was educated in France, where the sight of so many Frenchmen having their heads forcibly removed during the revolution left him with a lifelong revulsion of violence. In 1798 he was called to the bar, (that doesn't mean he went to the pub, but that he was officially made a barrister!). He married his third cousin,

Mary O'Connell, and they soon got down to business, producing no less than eleven offspring, seven of whom survived. O'Connell was horrified by the rebellion in 1798 and openly condemned Emmet's bloody rising in 1803, though he fully agreed with its aim of Catholic Emancipation. In 1815 O'Connell cast aspersions on Dublin Corporation, which at the time was a bastion of self-serving members of the Protestant Ascendancy. He refused to apologise for calling the Corpo 'beggarly' and was challenged to a duel by one of its members – Captain John D'Esterre. Captain D'Esterre was a well-known duellist so he

DUELLING POLITICAL PARTIES
SINN FÉIN V THE GREENS

was doubtless very surprised to be shot and killed by the pacifist O'Connell. The death horrified O'Connell, who paid an allowance to D'Esterre's daughter until the day he died. He vowed never to fight again, and when attending mass, he reputedly wore a black glove on his right hand as a symbol of his revulsion at all violence, which was a bit of a slap in the face for the armed rebels.

1823

The Catholic Association

While its name conjures up images of four-week retreats, fasting, confession and three-hour masses, this particular Catholic club actually had nothing to do with praising the Lord, thank God. O'Connell formed the Catholic Association with the aim of promoting Catholic Emancipation by legal and peaceful means. He charged just a penny for membership so that literally every poor sod in the country could afford to be a member. So many joined that the Association raised a gansey-load of dosh which was used to support the campaign for emancipation and also to help Catholic families who'd been evicted by rich landlords. The turning point for the Association came in 1828 when a by-election arose in County Clare. Due to a loophole in the law, while Catholics couldn't take a seat in the House of Commons, there was no law to say they couldn't stand for election (i.e. they could stand but not sit). O'Connell not only stood, he strolled it – and was duly elected.

Penny, circa 1828. O'Connell collected over eleven million of these while contesting the by-election in Clare

The Duke of Wellington

The largest obelisk in Europe is the Wellington Monument in Dublin's Phoenix Park, honouring Arthur Wellesley, Duke of Wellington. Famous as the man who defeated Napoleon at

Waterloo (well, him and an army of Prussians, who didn't have such good PR), Wellington was one of Britain's greatest generals and eventually became Prime Minister. He made the Wellington boot fashionable in his day and gave his name to it (but then some people still think Union Jack shorts are fashionable, so what can you expect?). Wellington was also Irish. Not exactly proud of his roots, he is supposed to have said of his birthplace that 'being born in a stable does not make one a horse.' Yeah, Arthur, and we've got somewhere you can stick Europe's largest obelisk.

The Wellington Monument in the Phoenix Park,
Dublin, erected in honour of some auld boot.

Cazholic Emancipazion

Prime Minister Wellesley (The Duke of Welling-ton) was afraid that if O'Connell wasn't allowed to take his seat, there could be an uprising and a great many of his buddies would have their arses kicked from here to kingdom come. So he decided to abolish virtually all anti-Catholic institutional discrimination. Naturally though, the English weren't going to break completely with hundreds of years of anti-Irish tradition, so Wellington, the old boot, scrapped the voting rights of £2 freeholders (raising it to a tenner!). This, in effect, meant that the vast majority of O'Connell's supporters couldn't vote. It was a bit like giving a starving man a roast chicken with the condition that he can't eat it. On the plus side, middle class Catholics could finally have careers in things like the Civil Service, the poor feckers. O'Connell's achievement in securing eman-cipation was a major breakthrough, and earned him the title 'The Liberator' in Ireland. O'Connell would also become the first Catholic in modern times to sit in the House of Commons.

The Night of the Big Wind

On the night of 6 January 1839, Ireland experienced possibly its worst storm in five hundred years. It is estimated that winds reached speeds of over 125 mph and caused damage to a quarter of all the buildings in the country, sank tens of ships and caused widespread flooding. Hundreds of people died and entire houses and factories were flattened, but at least one British army barracks was also flattened, so it wasn't all bad news. And you thought the wind was bad the night you had that hot curry!

1831

The Tithe War
Shooting themselves in the foot

Despite emancipation, the British decided to retain such practices as Catholics having to pay tithes – ten per cent of income from tillage farming had to be paid to the local Protestant minister. Not surprisingly, the Catholics found this a trifle annoying. Under O'Connell's stewardship they began a peaceful campaign of non-payment. The English responded by murdering them. Over the course of the war, which lasted almost a decade, there were many violent incidents, the most infamous being the massacre at Rathcormac in County Cork in 1837 where Archdeacon Ryder, on failing to get his four quid from a near-penniless old widow, gave his blessing to the soldiers to open fire, killing nine innocent people. The brave Archdeacon then seized a few bales of corn in lieu of payment. Realising that they were actually spending

FOR THE LOVE OF GOD MAN, STOP FIRING!
DON'T YOU REALISE HOW EXPENSIVE BULLETS ARE?

more in bullets than they were collecting in tithes, they finally conceded just a little. The tithe was reduced by a quarter and paid via the landlord, not directly to the Protestant church. Wow. One thing you can say about the Brits, they don't do things by halves, only quarters.

'There is no language like the Irish for soothing and quieting.'

——— *John Millington Synge, Irish Playwright and Poet, 1871–1909*

The Decline of the Irish Language

Although the Tudors had begun the process of killing off the Irish language, not to mention the Irish themselves, the real death knell for Irish was sounded with the introduction of the National Schools system in the 1830s. Under this system, children were regularly clattered senseless for speaking Irish. Ironically, a century later, when we'd won our freedom, the Christian Brothers reversed this policy and would clatter you senseless for *not* speaking Irish!

1838

The Poor Law

In England employment was on the increase and the government introduced the Poor Law as a means of encouraging people to work – the alternative to employment was to go to a workhouse, a place so grim not even an employee of a global burger chain would want to work there. In Ireland, the situation was different. There was very little employment and a commission had recommended strongly against implementing the same type of Poor Law here. So, as you might have come to expect by now, it went ahead and over a hundred workhouses were built, each with a capacity of 1,000 people. The residents were treated with complete brutality, and, hard as it is to believe, hygiene was worse than in the toilets of a Temple Bar pub on a Saturday night. Thousands never made it out of the workhouses alive, and considering what was on the way, they weren't going to be missing any fun times on the outside.

Fr Mathew's Temperance Crusade

Hordes of drunken lads lurching around ratarsed; fluthered, half-naked women roaming the streets. Sound familiar? No, not a 21st century Irish town on a weekend, but a scene from

170 years ago! Fr Theobald Mathew decided to do something about it and began his temperance movement, the Teetotal Abstinence Society. He managed to persuade a staggering 3 million people, half the population, to take 'The Pledge' – never to drink alcohol for the rest of their lives – and thereby stop them staggering. His movement spread all across England and the USA, where he was feted in the White House. Statues honour him in Cork and in Dublin's O'Connell Street, at the base of which you'll find a plastered-drunk youth puking on any given Friday night.

1840

O'Connell's Repeal Association

O'Connell believed that the only way to achieve significant rights for Catholics was the complete repeal of the Act of Union – we can run our own country, thanks very much. He set up the Repeal Association and gained the support of a newly emerging group called the Young Irelanders – young, educated radicals who would influence nationalist thinking for generations. In 1841, O'Connell took advantage of a change in the law to become the first Catholic Lord Mayor of Dublin since 1690, and for his troubles got himself a very nice gaff in Dawson Street – the Mansion House. His election helped to maintain his profile as Catholic Ireland's champion and in 1843 the subscriptions to his Repeal Association came to £48,400, which would barely cover a tribunal lawyer's wig expenses nowadays but back then helped provide enough funds for him to begin to organise his famous 'Monster Meetings' around the country.

'The altar of liberty totters when it is cemented only with blood.'

—— Daniel O'Connell, Irish Politician and Statesman, 1775-1847

O Connell's Monster Meetings

Traditionally held at Hallowe'en when the souls of the dead were reputed to wander the earth ... not really, but it does sound believable all the same! In fact, these were vast, peaceful meetings organised by

O'CONNELL'S MONSTER MEETING 1843

O'Connell to demonstrate to the British the strength of feeling about the Union in Ireland. And, sure enough, it wasn't long before the British were planking it, as crowds ranging from 100,000 to 750,000 attended meetings in places like Cashel, Kells and Tara – all venues carefully chosen by O'Connell because of their great historical significance to the Irish. He'd also planned for a meeting in Clontarf – site of Brian Boru's defeat of the Vikings. Sensing that history was about to repeat itself, the Brits sent in the artillery (the gathering crowds were all completely unarmed, but sure, that had never bothered them before). O'Connell was fearful of a massacre and at the last minute called off the meeting. Like a vast class of schoolchildren who'd just visited Dáil Éireann to see our leaders at work, the masses tramped home, utterly disillusioned.

1844

O Connell's Decline

It was the beginning of the end for O'Connell,

who was arrested for sedition (meaning 'speaking out against a bunch of oppressive bastards') and sentenced to a year in prison. He was released after three months. Despite his earlier successes, O'Connell's attempt to repeal the Act of Union failed and his health went into decline. The Great Famine would strike the following year and in his final speech to the House of Commons O'Connell pleaded for help for the Irish subjects of the crown – 'Ireland is in your hands ... she cannot save herself.'

In 1847, while on a pilgrimage to Rome, he died in Genoa. His heart was buried in Rome, his body in Glasnevin Cemetery in Dublin, where a huge round tower is built over his tomb. O'Connell was one of the first great leaders in world history to force political change entirely through peaceful means.

Dan the Man keeps vigil on O'Connell Street

The O'Connell Monument

The statue of Daniel O'Connell at the south end of O'Connell Street, Dublin was designed by John Henry Foley, one of the most famous sculptors of his day. He was also responsible for designing the Albert Memorial in London and well-known statues around the world, including one of the US Confederate General, 'Stonewall' Jackson in Virginia. In the 1970s some lune terrorist put a bomb at the base of the statue but only succeeded in sending one of the four angels around its base back to heaven. Other than that, Daniel the great pacifist was unmoved by the terrorist violence.

The Great Irish Famine

The famine that struck Ireland in late 1845 was without doubt the greatest catastrophe to befall Ireland in her history. It claimed more than one million lives – over one eight of the population; another million and a half were forced to emigrate. Its causes were two-fold. One was natural, the other was British-made. Because the impoverished farmers had to pay inflated rents to their mostly British landlords, the only way to feed their families was to rely on the potato, which had a very high yield. When potato blight struck in September 1845 and again in the four succeeding years, the outcome was predictable. People began to starve. They died in their thousands. Disease was rampant. But hang on – Irish people were subjects of the crown, so Queen Victoria and her government were surely going to step in and save the Irish from such a hideous fate? They were in their arse.

The haunting Famine Memorial at the Custom
House, Dublin, by sculptor Rowan Gllespie.

Famine Relief

In 1846 the British Prime Minister, John Russell, entrusted Sir Charles Edward Trevelyan with the task of co-ordinating famine relief. This was akin to appointing a Japanese trawler harpoonist to head a 'Save the Whale' committee. Both men firmly believed that you shouldn't interfere in a country's economy because it inhibited private enterprise. Which is funny, because they'd made sure Scotland had plenty of food when the blight hit there! It just happens they were disciples of an economist called John Malthus, who believed that famine should be facilitated to eradicate 'excess population'. Trevelyan actually once said that the famine was 'a direct stroke of an all-wise and all-merciful Providence', presumably on the basis that it got rid of so many pesky Paddies. Hardly Mother Teresa, was he? By the way, if you've ever sung 'The Fields of Athenry' – and who hasn't – this is the same Trevelyan whose corn has been stolen in the song.

'I would walk from here to Drogheda and back to see the man who is blockhead enough to expect anything except injustice from an English Parliament.'

— *Daniel O'Connell, Irish Politician and Statesman, 1775-1847*

1845 – 1860

Mass Emigration

The stench of death hung over the entire country. The nauseous smell of the blackened, withered potato plants combined with the stink of corpses rotting in the open countryside. The disease-ridden workhouses were overflowing and the only option left to millions was emigration, mostly to America and Canada, but also to cities like Liverpool in northern England and Glasgow in Scotland. Unfortunately, the ships used to transport the thousands who left each day were often unseaworthy or overcrowded. Many perished in the Atlantic, some not even making it out of the harbour. Others were forced to endure the entire crossing below deck where disease was rampant, and the new life many dreamed of died with them before they ever reached port. The ships were known as coffin ships. The owners usually made a killing in more ways than one.

INTERESTING STUFF

A helping hand from the Choctaw Indians.

In the middle of the famine, a group of Choctaw Indians, (from the south east coast of the US) decided to try to raise funds for famine relief in Ireland. Sixteen years previously they had faced starvation themselves during their forcible re-location from Mississhippi to Oklahoma – a walk of 500 miles, which had been called the 'Trail of Tears'. They were clearly keen not to see others undergo the same fate. This impoverished people managed to raise a staggering $710 – which would be the equivalent of around a million dollars today. To mark the 150th anniversary of their great humanitarian gesture, eight Irish people retraced the Trail of Tears .

The long-terms effects of the Great Famine

It is estimated that the population of Ireland was approximately nine million in 1845. The census of 1861 counted six and a half million. Sir Charles Trevelyan must have been delighted that God's plan had worked out so well. Over the coming decades further losses through emigration or death through deprivation would reduce the population to a mere four million. The vast loss of life left deep emotional scars on the minds of many and would influence nationalist thinking and attitudes towards Britain for generations to come – right up to the present day, in fact.

'The starlight of heaven above us shall quiver. As our souls flow in one down eternity's river.'

———————— *Thomas Davis, Irish Politician and Writer, 1814-1845*

1840 – 1900

The Nation

The *Nation* newspaper was founded by a group of young intellectuals – Thomas Davis, John Blake Dillon and Charles Gavan Duffy – with the aim of promoting Irish nationalism and having the Act of Union revoked. These men, some Protestant and others Catholic, became known as the Young Irelanders because of their youthful enthusiasm and idealism (Duffy was just 27, Davis & Dillon 29). The *Nation* attracted a brilliant group of writers and poets who began to restore pride in Irish language, literature, culture and history. It was also ahead of its time in employing women writers, albeit under male pseudonyms, because Irish men didn't take orders from any woman – except their mothers, wives and girlfriends, that is. One of those women writers, incidentally, was Oscar Wilde's mother.

The Irish Tricolour

The French Revolution of 1848 had just taken place when Young Irelander Thomas Francis Meagher visited Paris to get some revolutionary tips. He was inspired by the French red, white and blue tricolour. So, that March in Waterford, he unfurled what was to become the Irish national flag – vertical green, white and orange – from the window of a house. Green represented Catholics, Orange represented Protestants and white the peace between them. Meagher's father had been born in Newfoundland whose flag was a green, white and pink tricolour. Pink wasn't Thomas's favourite colour, thanks be to Jaysus.

Young Irelander Rebellion

Two of the most prominent Young Irelanders were William Smith O'Brien and Thomas Francis Meagher. They decided it was time to take up arms.

The problem was that most of their rebel 'army' were so malnourished they barely had the strength to take up knitting, never mind arms. As a result, the only serious 'battle' of the rebellion happened in the village of Ballingarry, in Tipperary, where the rebels had set up barricades. The police (who were Irishmen loyal to Britain), approached and decided to take refuge in a large house owned by the widow McCormack. They also took Mrs McCormack's five children hostage. When the house was surrounded by the rebels and O'Brien tried to negotiate with the police, they shot him, but only succeeded in wounding him. Eventually, after some skirmishing, a number of the rebels lay dead and the police couldn't be shifted. Police reinforcements soon arrived and the rebels legged it. The 'rebellion' was over almost before it started. The leaders were initially sentenced to death but this was commuted to exile to Van Diemen's Land, from where most of them escaped to America. Ha ha.

INTERESTING STUFF

Charles Gavan Duffy

Having taken on the British establishment here, Young Irelander Charles Gavan Duffy left

Ireland in 1856, a disillusioned man, and emigrated to Australia, where he duly took on the British establishment there, and became (Catholic) Premier of Victoria in 1871, much to the disgust of the Protestant establishment.

1866

The Fenian Brotherhood and the Canadian Plan
Africans and Indians join the Irish

The Fenian Brotherhood was founded in the United States by ex-Young Irelander John O'Mahoney. The word 'Fenian' was derived from the ancient Irish warriors know as the Fianna, in mythology led by Fionn Mac Cumhaill. Unfortunately, one of their schemes for the freeing of Ireland would have required some of Fionn's legendary magic to succeed. This was a daring plan to invade British-occupied Canada, seize or disrupt its transportation network of ships and trains and, in effect, set up an 'Overseas Republic of Ireland'. In total they made five raids and, with the exception of a minor victory at Ridgeway near Niagara Falls, were largely unsuccessful. One interesting sidenote was that the Fenian ranks included 500 Mohawk Indians and one company of 100 African-American veterans of the Union Army! Was there anyone on earth that didn't have a bone to pick with the British?

INTERESTING STUFF

'A Nation Once Again'

This famous Irish song was written by Young Irelander Thomas Davis, one of the men most responsible for promoting the idea of Irish nationalism among the great unwashed. In 2002, in a BBC Global Service poll, his 'A Nation Once Again' was voted The World's Most Popular Song! Seems everyone with a drop of Irish blood must have voted for it. Which when you think about it, *is* pretty much everyone.

The Fenian Rising

Unfortunately for the Fenians, they weren't very good at organising. Their planned rising was originally intended for 11 February 1867, but because half their leaders were under arrest, they postponed it until March. Sadly, because mobile phone coverage was notoriously bad in the West, word failed to reach Cork and Kerry, and Fenians there went ahead. Poorly armed and badly organised, they quickly had the crap kicked out of them. When the rescheduled rising happened in March, the leaders realised that their 'oath-bound secret society' was riddled with gougers who couldn't even spell oath and whose notion of secrecy was not to tell the wife. As a result, virtually everywhere

UH OH.

the Rising went ahead – eg Tallaght, Sligo, Limerick, Tipp and Louth, the rebels found themselves confronted by armed and waiting British soldiers – and some of the poor eejits were only armed with hurleys, which might be deadly weapons in Croker, but were not very effective against a 50lb cannonball. To cap it all, there was a snowstorm that night. They should have used the snowballs!

1867

The Manchester Martyrs

Several of the Fenian leaders were in prison in England, and while two of them (Colonel Thomas J Kelly and Captain Tim Deasy) were being transported to a kangaroo court for trial, their comrades mounted a rescue attempt. Unfortunately, when they tried to shoot the lock off the door, they accidentally killed the guard inside. Kelly and Deasy escaped to America but three others were later arrested and sentenced to death for murder. It mattered not that William Allen,

Monument to the Manchester Martyrs
in, of all places, Manchester.

Michael Larkin, and William O'Brien hadn't fired the shot, the 'innocent until proven Irish' rule applied. The execution of the three became a symbol of injustice for generations of republicans to come.

Manchester Martyrs Monuments
Allen, Larkin and O'Brien have a dispropor-tionate number of monuments in their name – a couple in Clare, one in Limerick, Dublin, Tipperary, Offaly and Manchester – almost more than any of the great Irish leaders in history!

1868

William Gladstone

There was one good thing about elections in those days – you weren't tortured by party political broadcasts. When Gladstone was elected Prime Minister he decided he was going to try to settle what was known at the time as 'The Irish Question', the question as far as the Irish were concerned being, 'Why doesn't Britain get the f**k out of Ireland?' Anyway, Gladstone wasn't such a bad old sort, which made a welcome change. For starters he decided to disestablish the Church of Ireland, officially breaking the link between the church and the state, which is never a bad idea. Gladstone also introduced two Land Acts, one of which guaranteed the 'Three Fs': fixity of tenure, fair rents and free sale. While Gladstone's efforts did bring some relief to Irish tenant farmers, most were still existing in brutal conditions.

1868 AND IRISH FARMERS COME UP WITH A MORE APPROPRIATE "F" FOR ENGLISH PARLIMENT.

'We are bound to lose Ireland in
consequence of years of cruelty,
stupidity and misgovernment and
I would rather lose her as a
friend than as a foe.'

William E. Gladstone, British Prime Minister, 1809-1898

1870 – 1874

The Home Rule League
You want WHAT?

Nowadays, young American visitors to Dublin like to amuse themselves by bending over the rail on Butt Bridge in Dublin and having a picture taken of their extensive arses, which they then show to their friends at home with great mirth. The unfortunately named Isaac Butt founded the Home Rule League in 1870, its aims being pretty clear from its name, and in the 1874 election the League won fifty-nine seats. With all those Isaac Butt butts on seats in the British

Parliament, they employed the tactic of filibustering. This sounds like some sort of deviant nineteenth century sexual practice, but it simply meant that they kept talking and talking and talking during a debate until the time allotted ran out, thus preventing the Brits from passing any laws in their own country and keeping Irish issues top of the agenda. It also had the effect of boring the English to tears, which serves them bloody right, as they've been doing this to everyone else on the planet for centuries.

BRITISH PARLIAMENT HARD AT WORK. 1870S

INTERESTING STUFF

A Bridge Not Too Far
Butt Bridge is the only stone bridge across the Liffey that was actually named after the person for whom it was intended (in 1879, when Isaac Butt died). All the others were inherited from

the British and immediately renamed after Irish heroes. Those bridges are O'Connell Bridge (formerly Carlisle), O'Donovan Rossa Bridge (formerly Richmond), Fr Mathew Bridge (formerly Whitworth), Queen Maeve Bridge (formerly named Queen's Bridge, after Charlotte, wife of George III) and Grattan Bridge (formerly Essex).

1874 – 1880

Charles Stewart Parnell

When Butt died, Parnell succeeded him as leader of the Home Rule Party. Born in County Wicklow, Parnell was a Protestant of aristocratic background and was to become one of the most influential figures in Irish history. Gladstone called him the most remarkable person he'd ever met, future PM Asquith called him one of the greatest figures of the 19th century, and the Catholic Church called him everything under the sun that they could without using swear words (for reasons which will be obvious later). Parnell's genius was his organisational skill, and before long he'd united the factions within his party with an oath of loyalty and using a strict party Whip. He also gave the boot to landlords and Tory supporters from the organisation as they were part of the old Protestant Ascendancy and weren't always in agreement with the party aims of getting rid of the old Protestant Ascendancy. Parnell's Irish Parliamentary Party became the model for all modern British political parties. And it is certainly true that one or two Tory MPs do like a good whip.

1879

The Land League

The winter of 1878-79 was particularly bitter and many farmers were terrified that another famine was looming. Michael Davitt, a former Fenian recently released from jail in England, was also feeling fairly frosty towards the landed classes, so he organised a protest in his home county of Mayo that April against one particular offending landlord, Canon Geoffrey

Bourke, a man of the cloth, no less. Confronted by thousands of hungry Mayo savages, the good Canon suddenly discovered the benefits to the body and soul

of the Christian act and promptly reduced his rents by 25% and withdrew all his eviction notices. Davitt soon realised that his and Parnell's goals were as one and in October that year they teamed up to form the Land League. Unfortunately for the landlords, this was not a hurling competition between teams of local farmers, but a way of organising tenant farmers, getting fair rents and providing support for those who'd been evicted. Support in this instance was actual money, rather than yelling 'C'mon ye boys in green'. Davitt and Parnell had recently toured America, seen the sights and came back with about thirty grand in the form of donations from Irish emigrants.

Parnell pointing the way forward,
O'Connell Street, Dublin.

Origin of the word 'boycott'

When Captain Charles Boycott, the land agent for the absentee landlord Earl Erne, refused to lower his rents, Parnell encouraged the community to ostracise him. Work stopped in his fields, shopkeepers wouldn't sell his goods, his mail didn't arrive and, worst of all, the pub wouldn't sell him any drink. Eventually the British supplied a force of 1,000 soldiers to protect fifty Orangemen who were brought in to harvest his crops. This cost twenty-five times the value of the crop, so it wasn't exactly a great investment. And he was still treated like an outcast when they'd gone! Within the year he was gone, too.

1880 – 1882

The Land Wars

A bit of a misnomer, really. Far from encouraging the slaughter of the poor innocent landlords, the

Land League encouraged peaceful resistance through protest, mutual support and boycotts. As the months passed, however, the organised resistance to the landlords saw rural Ireland drifting into chaos, much like it is on Friday nights after the pubs close. Forcible evictions and the burning of homes became commonplace. The landlords were supported by the constabulary which was bitterly resented as most of these men were Irish, and there were deaths on both sides. The British answer to this was to arrest Parnell, an action which, predictably, made Parnell a national hero and galvanised the protesting farmers. He was sent to Kilmainham Goal, but before you could say 'No U-

CANCEL MY TWELVE O'CLOCK, MRS MURPHY, I HAVE TO MEET THE PRIME MINISTER

turns' the British were back negotiating with him in jail. He successfully negotiated a revised Second Land Bill with Gladstone which offered Irish farmers a much better deal. This became known as the Kilmainham Treaty and, as a 'treaty' is normally an agreement between countries, this was the first subconscious British acknowledgement that Ireland was moving ever more slowly towards nationhood. And about bleedin' time.

The Phoenix Park Murders
Invincibles, my arse!

Things were coming together nicely. And then, as is common the world over, a bunch of mentallers – in our case called 'The Invincibles' – screw it up for everyone. This extremist nationalist faction didn't believe in holding talks with anyone, probably not even each other. Just four days after Parnell was released from Kilmainham, they decided to murder the Permanent Under-Secretary for Ireland, Thomas

Henry Burke and the Chief Secretary, Lord Cavendish, who'd had the bad luck to arrive in the country that very day. Instead of the Céad Mile Fáilte he'd been led to expect by the Tourist Board, he and Burke were attacked and stabbed to death in the Phoenix Park, just a short walk from their residence. The murders were big news all across Europe, and in Britain there was outrage. Parnell condemned the murders, but the damage had been done, especially as one of Gladstone's chief supporters happened to be Cavendish's big brother, who immediately withdrew his support. The prospects for Home Rule suddenly seemed a long way from home. Five of 'The Invincibles' were hanged for the murders, thereby proving their gang's name to have been slightly optimistic, to say the least.

WHO...PICKED... THIS...STUPID...NAME ... ANYWAY????

A walk in the park

The Phoenix Park in Dublin is the largest walled city park in Europe and contains Áras an Uachtaráin – the residence of the President of Ireland, The Wellington Monument, The Papal Cross (where Pope John Paul celebrated mass to one million people in 1979), The US Ambassador's residence and Dublin Zoo. The Irish State guest house, Farmleigh, adjoins the park, where foreign dignitaries come to see Irish politicians, much the same way people come to visit the orang-utang enclosure in Dublin Zoo.

1884

The Gaelic Athletic Association
The Road to Croker

The GAA was founded by Michael Cusack in County Tipperary in 1884, although the earliest recorded Gaelic football match took place at Slane in County Meath in 1712, when Meath played their neighbours, Louth. This was the last time Louth actually won a match. The GAA's aims were to revitalise interest in traditional Irish sports like hurling, Gaelic football, camogie, handball and kicking the Brits out of Ireland. And very successful they were; 125 years on there are almost a million members of the association, of whom about 250,000 actually play and the rest come along for the cheap drink in the clubhouse. Croke Park is the jewel in the GAA's crown, the largest amateur sports stadium in the world, with a capacity of 80,000. And recently the GAA hardliners finally relented and allowed the foreign (British) sports of soccer and rugby to be played in 'Croker', thereby finally bringing those diehards into the 20th century. Unfortunately for them it's now the 21st century.

SUPPOSE IT MADE A CHANGE FROM FIGHTING WITH THE BRITS.

1886

Gladstone's Home Rule Bill

Prime Minister Gladstone believed it was a moral imperative that Ireland should have Home Rule, but he knew the very thought of it would upset lots of people. His opponents saw it as a slippery slope – give Ireland Home Rule and all the other nations around the globe that they'd trampled on, exploited and mistreated would want the same! The nerve! For these reasons Gladstone worked on the Bill in complete secrecy. When he finally revealed his grand design, nobody was impressed. Britain would retain control of trade, defence, war and peace issues, money and the police (although the Dubs would get their own police force). That would leave an Irish Parliament with only enough power to open a bag of crisps, which was far too much for Gladstone's opponents, especially the Unionists in Northern Ireland. Parnell reluctantly gave it his support, as he saw it as a first step. But the Bill was defeated and Unionist supporters in Belfast enjoyed some deadly celebrations, literally, their exuberance resulting in the deaths of eight Catholics.

The Defeat of Gladstone

To Unionists in Ulster, Gladstone was like the Pope in disguise. They believed that Home Rule would mean an end to their privileged position, and they were right. Many of Gladstone's opponents saw this as an opportunity to undermine further the PM's position. One of these, Tory MP Randolph Churchill (Winston's Da), decided to lend the Unionists his support, declaring famously that 'Ulster will fight and Ulster will be right'.

This statement ignored the fact that Ulster was half Catholic, and that half of the Home Rule leadership had been Protestants. It also set the trend for snappy Unionist slogans, being followed soon after by 'Home Rule means Rome Rule'. There was also 'Ulster says No', 'Never, never, never, never!' and 'Set Fenians alight, we don't give a shite!' The upshot of all this was that Gladstone was booted out at the next election and the Conservatives came to power. Being Conservatives, they conserved. In other words, nothing changed. It was a bitter disappointment for

Parnell, but he'd soon have other things on his mind, anyway

The Piggott Forgeries

In 1887, The *Times* newspaper printed a series of articles accusing Parnell of supporting the murders in the Phoenix Park. These were based on letters Parnell supposedly wrote. However, a Commission of Enquiry found that the letters had been forged by *Times*' journalist Richard Piggott. He was caught rapid because of his poor spelling. Among the errors was the word 'hesitancy' spelled 'hesitency' and the phrase 'I'm a forging bleedin' bastard' in which 'bastard' was spelled 'barstarred'. This one slipped by the editor, though, and The *Times* had to fork out £5,000 to Parnell – an enormous amount at the time. Piggot duly legged it to Madrid and blew out what little brains he had. A century later The *Times* would print 'The Hitler Diaries'...

The Fall of Parnell

The seeds of Parnell's downfall would be sown in 1880, not by fervent Unionists or looney Tories or hard-line Republicans, but by something much more scary. A feckin' woman! This was the year Parnell met and fell head over heels in love with Katherine 'Kitty' O'Shea. And she with him. The only problem was the lovely Kitty was already hitched to one Captain O'Shea, who was actually a Home Ruler, but clearly didn't rule much in his own home. In fact, it's widely believed he knew his missus was playing away from home with his boss, but because Parnell had him elected in Galway in 1886, and with the prospect of a large bequest from Kitty's aunt, he kept his trap shut. When the bequest didn't happen, O'Shea spilled the beans, opened a can of worms and let the kitty out of the bag all in one go. All hell broke loose when O'Shea filed for divorce and named Parnell in the proceedings. The Catholic church condemned Parnell roundly, the Unionists used it to highlight their moral superiority (so at least it gave us one good laugh) and the press had a field day. Parnell's party split when he refused to resign, but Parnell continued to campaign. He eventually married Kitty in 1891, but their marriage was brief. He died of pneumonia in October 1891, aged

just forty-five. His funeral was the largest Dublin had ever seen, with a quarter of a million people, both Protestant and Catholic, lining the streets. It was remarked by some women that it was the first time they'd ever seen their men crying. (The next time would be when Italy knocked Ireland out of Italia '90.) He is buried in Glasnevin Cemetery, his headstone reading simply 'Parnell'.

Conradh na Gaeilge (The Gaelic League)

Irish as a spoken language was in decline. This was because it's difficult to speak Irish when you're dead, as was the case with so many people as a result of the Great Famine. Many other native Irish speakers had been forced to emigrate to America, and it was too hard to hear them from there. So a group was formed in July 1893 specifically to promote the speaking of the Irish language, or, as we say today, to use the 'cúpla focal' (pronounced coo-pla fuck-al, meaning the couple of words of Irish). Its principal founder was Douglas Hyde, who would later become Ireland's first President. Conradh na Gaeilge, which is still in existence, had a large degree of success and over the decades the number of Irish speakers gradually climbed. For ages they were easily recognised by their unpronounceable surnames and hairy beards, but the gorgeous Gaeilgeoir weather girls on TG4 have made us look at Irish in a completely new way. Go háilinn! Incidentally, the group's first newspaper was edited by Padraig Pearse and was called 'The Sword of Light'. This would later be called a Light Sabre and be Luke Skywalker's weapon of choice in *Star Wars*.

INTERESTING STUFF

Percy French and the West Clare Railway

Famous as the composer of many Irish standards like 'The Mountains of Mourne' and 'Come back Paddy Reilly to Ballyjamesduff', French also wrote the ditty 'Are ye right there Michael' after a notoriously long trip on the West Clare Railway line left him late for a gig. The song ridiculed the train service (imagine the material he'd have with our current Health Service!) and he subsequently brought an action for loss of earnings against the company. Legend has it he arrived late for the hearing, his excuse being he'd travelled on the West Clare Railway, at which the judge promptly awarded him £10 in damages!

The Second Home Rule Bill

Round Two

Proving that you can't keep a good man down – especially when he's on Viagra – good old Gladstone was returned to power in Britain for the fourth time at the age of eighty-three. He immediately set about getting Home Rule back on track and the Unionists just as quickly set about causing a high speed derailment. The Bill would give Ireland a sort of regional assembly, hardly a parliament at all, but even that was too much

GLADSTONE 4

HE'S BACK!
AND THIS TIME
IT'S PERSONAL

for the Unionists in Northern Ireland, who were becoming increasingly separatist from the rest of the island of Ireland and whose latest slogan was 'They're our bag of sweets and we're not sharing them'. The Bill was passed by the House of Commons. Unfortunately it was defeated in the House of Lords, which was populated mainly by stuffy old Tory farts, most of whom were as lordly as a cowpat. It was the end for Gladstone. He resigned a few months later and died in 1898. Years later, King George V would say 'What fools we were not to pass Mr Gladstone's Bill when we had the chance!' Well duuuuh.

'All the world's a stage and most of us are desperately unrehearsed.'

Sean O'Casey, Irish Playwright, 1880-1964

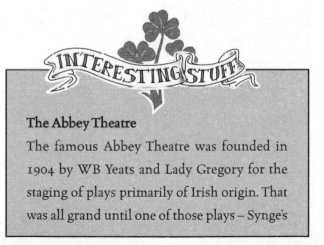

The Abbey Theatre

The famous Abbey Theatre was founded in 1904 by WB Yeats and Lady Gregory for the staging of plays primarily of Irish origin. That was all grand until one of those plays – Synge's

'Playboy of the Western World' caused riots because it cast a 'slight on the virtue of Irish womanhood'. The press slated the rioters – probably because many an Irish woman's virtue was actually slight. The original quaint theatre building burned down in 1951 only to be replaced by an eyesore in 1966. The plays performed within, by contrast, are still a sight for sore eyes.

1890 – 1925

The Celtic Literary Renaissance
Write Here, Write Now

During this turbulent period in Irish history, (as opposed to the turbulent period that had existed for the past 800 years), there was one glimmer of brightness to lighten the seemingly unrelenting bad news. Around this time a whole gansey-load of significant writers began to emerge: WB Yeats, George Russell, Oliver St John Gogarty, Lady Gregory, JM Synge, Sean O'Casey. And ever after Ireland would be known as a land of writers, which is a lot better than being known as a land of corrupt politicians, endless tribunals, high prices and shite weather. Much of the writing during this period was influenced by ancient Irish mythology and folklore and this helped to strengthen the nation's sense of their unique Irish identity. And, yes, we still believe all the myths about ourselves!

CUCHULAINN, IRELAND'S LEGENDARY WARRIOR, HAD TO ADMIT THE PEN WAS INDEED MIGHTIER THAN THE SWORD

Monto

Immortalised by The Dubliners in the song 'Take her up to Monto', this was Dublin's famous red light district, which got its name from Montgomery Street (now Foley Street). At the turn of the century it was Europe's largest red light district, with as many as 1,500 ladies selling their wares there. Among those reputed to purchase those wares were the then Prince of Wales, who regularly had his royal sceptre polished there. The Catholic Church eventually closed down most of the brothels as they needed to get some of their priests back saying mass.

I'M NOT SURE WHY, BUT I'VE ALWAYS HAD A SOFT SPOT FOR THE MONTO AREA OF DUBLIN?

The Local Government (Ireland) Act

The first significant concession from the British Parliament in terms of Irish self-government for donkey's years. The Act introduced us to the wonderful world of county councils, allowing us for the first time to directly elect our own crooked councillors, as opposed to crooked councillors loyal to Britain. From this day forth we'd be fully entitled to elect officials in our own local areas so that they could waste the taxpayers' money arranging useless 'twinning' projects with towns in France, Spain, Italy etc that had absolutely no connection with us whatsoever – some of them didn't even possess a pub! – just so they could go on 'free' junkets abroad, instead of their usual trip to Ballybunion. On the other hand, at long last Ireland had a bunch of people we could blame for making a pig's arse of a situation who weren't British.

VOTE No. 1

SEAN "I'LL SEE YOU RIGHT" MURPHY

The Limerick Pogrom

Not quite as dramatic as the name suggests, thanks be to Jaysus, as there was no actual violence involved, but Limerick's proud history was sadly tainted by this shameful event. In 1904, a Catholic priest, Fr John Creagh, began ranting from the pulpit in a very un-Christian way about how the city's tiny population of Jews (mostly traders) were an economic blight on the Christian poor, the killers of Christ, blah bollox blah shite blah. Only the local police prevented a mob from probably crucifying a few Jews. A two-year boycott of Jews ensued and virtually all of them fled to America or to Cork, where they were accepted. The son of one of these refugees, Gerald Goldberg, eventually became Cork's first Jewish Lord Mayor in 1977.

LORD I KNOW WE'RE THE CHOSEN PEOPLE... BUT COULD YOU CHOOSE SOMEONE ELSE FOR A CHANGE?

General Elections in Britain

After over five years in power, the anti-Ireland party, oops, sorry, the Tories, had their arses kicked in the general election, losing over 250 seats. Wondrous as this news initially sounded to Irish ears, unfortunately it left the Liberals in an unassailable position which meant that they could carry on the long British tradition of ignoring Ireland's needs and problems.

SORRY CHAPS. IT WOULD APPEAR WE'VE LOST SOME SEATS. I DON'T SUPPOSE YOU'VE SEEN THEM?

During their term they did indirectly manage one favour for Ireland, taking away the right of the House of Lords to block legislation. Four years later there was another election and the Tories managed to regain many of their lost seats, but not quite enough. It meant that the Liberals needed the help of the Irish Parliamentary Party, under John Redmond, to hold on to power. Of course there'd be a price for his help … Home Rule for Ireland.

The Rise of Unionism in Ireland

Home Rule was knocking on the door. But behind that door were thousands of Ulster Unionists waiting to blow it to pieces the moment the door was opened. Their leader was Edward Carson, a barrister from Dublin, who believed wholeheartedly that the union with Britain was to everyone in Ireland's benefit ... well certainly everyone Protestant at least. A brilliant orator, Carson was invited to be the leader of the Unionist Party and he accepted, despite having reservations – he was a Dub, had no direct connection with Ulster Protestants and thought Orangemen were a right shower of savages. He was also in favour of all of Ireland – not just Ulster – remaining within the Union. Nevertheless he took up the cause and spoke forcibly against the third Home Rule Bill in the House of Commons. When that didn't work, in 1913 he organised Ireland's first paramilitary force – The Ulster Volunteer Force. The following year the German Kaiser kindly supplied them with a huge shipment of German arms. He'd generously supply their opponents in the south with more arms soon after. Seems the ol' Kaiser was always keen to stir the shit in Ireland in the hope that some of it would splash on Britain.

INTERESTING STUFF

The Titanic

You know how the story ended – the world's biggest ocean liner at the time, sank after striking an iceberg on its maiden voyage in the mid-Atlantic on April 15th, 1912 with the loss of over 1,500 lives. But the story actually began with the construction of the ship in the Harland & Wolff shipyard in Belfast. Designed by an Irishman and built by thousands of Irish engineers and labourers in an Irish shipyard, the Titanic had one major design flaw – it was being steered by an Englishman! No, only kidding! The terrible fact is that if the Titanic had hit the iceberg head-on instead of trying to steer around it, fewer sections of the ship would have been breached and in all probability it would have stayed afloat!

The Third Home Rule Bill

In September 1912 over a quarter of a million Protestants had signed the Ulster Covenant, essentially vowing loyalty to the King. In other words opposing what they saw as the awful prospect of rule by the evil demons in the South. Nevertheless, after all sorts of dramas, technical problems and a cast of thousands, finally in 1914, "Home Rule 3" was finally about to open in a Parliament near you. Then that damn Bosnian - Herzegovinian would go and shoot bleedin' Archduke Franz Ferdinand!!! Yep, the whole shebang was postponed due to World War 1.

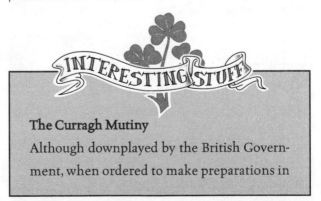

INTERESTING STUFF

The Curragh Mutiny
Although downplayed by the British Government, when ordered to make preparations in

1914 to go up to Ulster and put down those in-
fernal, armed Ulster Unionists should they vi-
olently oppose Home Rule, fifty British officers
at the Curragh Army base in Kildare resigned.
This was the single biggest mutiny of officers
in the history of the British armed forces. The
Government backed down, which told nationalists what they already knew – they had as
much chance of being treated impartially as a
one-legged man has in an
arse kicking contest.

ARSE
KICKING

1908 – 1914

The Birth of Trade Unionism in Ireland

In 1910 the price of a pint of porter was
roughly the equivalent of two cents in today's money.

Brilliant, you think, let's all timewarp back to 1913. For the price of a single pint nowadays you could have enjoyed 200 back then, roughly the equivalent of what a bunch of present-day skangers drink on an average Friday night. The only problem was that the ordinary worker was paid  around a pound (1.27 Euro) a week, from which he had to pay rent and feed and clothe his family, usually leaving his disposable income at minus thruppence halfpenny. Most workers' families lived in filthy slums and as there was an oversupply of labour they had to compete for work. The employers naturally exploited this by reducing pay and making them work up to eighteen hours a day (and you thought having to work until seven was a pain). Appalled by these conditions, James Connolly, an Edinburgh-born socialist, and Jim Larkin, a Liverpool-born socialist, formed the Irish Transport and General Workers Union and began to organise strike action, enjoying a number of successes. It was only a matter of time before the employers struck back.

Big Jim Larkin, Giving it his all on O'Connell Street.

1913 – 1914

The Dublin Lockout

The employers' leader was William Martin Murphy, or William 'Murder' Murphy as he became known. He was a filthy-rich businessman, owner of the Dublin United Tramway Company, Clery's Department Store and founder of the *Irish Independent* and *Evening Herald* newspapers which he used to attack Larkin and Connolly. The *Indo* and *Herald* were filled with inaccurate and one-sided bilge about absolutely nothing. And that was just last weekend. Back in 1913 it was nearly as bad. Murphy decided to fire anyone who was in the union and Larkin responded by calling a strike on 26 August – during the Dublin Horse Show, thereby denying rich people their most basic need – sitting around on their arses doing nothing while being served cocktails. Murphy and his cronies (some 300 fellow employers) hit back by locking out their employees, aiming to defeat them through starvation. In the months that followed, violence erupted frequently, especially when blackleg labour was used, and in one major incident, when Larkin was addressing the crowd in O'Connell Street, the good old Dublin Metropolitan Police decided to baton charge. Two men died, hundreds were injured. Eventually the strike was defeated in early 1914. Skeletal workers limped back under the gaze of gloating employers. But they knew they'd been in a fight. Many had been driven almost to bankruptcy and they wouldn't be in a hurry to take on the union again any time soon.

1907 – 1913

Thomas Clarke and the Irish Republican Brotherhood

Although originally founded by James Stephens

sixty years earlier, the IRB had no significant influence on Ireland's fight for independence. Not yet anyway. But its nationalist Gaelic ideals hadn't been forgotten. Thomas Clarke was a veteran Fenian who had learned to use explosives while blasting a tunnel on Staten Island. He now turned his skills to blasting a bridge – London Bridge to be exact. He was caught and spent fifteen years in prison. Not exactly a fan of the British after his time in the slammer, he returned to Ireland in 1907 and opened a tobacco shop, no doubt hoping the English soldiers he sold his products to would die

of raging emphysema. In 1913 he decided to revitalise the spirit of the IRB and began a recruitment drive. Not at liberty to run a nationwide ad campaign with a

catchy jingle, he mostly recruited from the then political and peaceful movement which had been founded
by Arthur Griffith. It was called Sinn Féin.

The Irish Volunteers
There's a First Time for Everything!

Percy French's song, 'Phil the Fluter's Ball',
was extremely popular around this time. Next most
popular thing was forming your own army. The IRB
was back in business, James Connolly had his Citizen's Army to protect workers, up in Ulster the UVF
were volunteering in force, and not to be outdone, nationalists in the south, like Patrick Pearse, Seán Mac
Diarmada and Eamonn Ceannt, decided to form the
Irish Volunteers to counter the threat from the boyos
up north. At their first meeting, thousands packed
the Rotunda in Dublin, the only objector being the
woman who was giving birth at the time. When WWI
broke out, the leader of the Irish Parliamentary Party,
John Redmond, wanted the Volunteers to fight for the
British against Germany, hoping that their allegiance

would ensure the implementation of Home Rule. But the Irish Volunteers had been infiltrated by the IRB and the chances of them supporting the British were about the same as a Fianna Fáil infrastructure project coming in under budget: absolutely zilch.

Irish soldiers in WWI

Although conscription wasn't introduced to Ireland during World War I, thousands of Irishmen from the south joined up (many through want of work). Here, ironically, they found themselves fighting alongside the very guys they would have happily shot a few weeks before – UVF men from Ulster. Estimates put the war losses of Irish soldiers from north and south at between 40,000-50,000.

Halfway through the war Britain finds a novel way to get more Irishmen to enlist

Gun-running at Howth

Seafront Attractions

The IRB felt a sudden emotional bond with *Die Fatherland* and managed to arrange a shipment of about 1,000 rifles (the Kaiser was now supplying the Unionist and the Nationalists!) which were brought into Howth in Dublin on the Asgard by Erskine Childers – a wealthy English Protestant member of the Royal Navy! (*see box*). Having successfully landed the arms and done a spot of windsurfing, Childers and the other Volunteers were met by the British Army on the way back into Dublin. They escaped, but a crowd of un-armed civilian supporters heckled the British. Being unfamiliar with the old Irish tradition of slagging, the army naturally opened fire and killed four people. This act, combined with the fact that the UVF had been openly allowed ship in enough guns to start a war against China, brought a surge in the numbers of Volunteers across the country.

The Riddle of Erskine Childers

An English Protestant, Childers had been a Lieutenant Commander in the Royal Navy, was a British Army veteran, awarded the DSC for bravery and he finally ended up as a nationalist gun-runner! But before he did all that he had time to write what has been called the first spy thriller, *The Riddle of the Sands*. The book accurately predicted a British war with Germany and Churchill credited it as his reason for establishing naval bases on Britain's east coast. Before WWI the book was hugely popular in Britain. Ironically, having turned his back on the country of his birth, he was executed by Irishmen – Free State forces – during the civil war. His son, also Erskine Childers, was President of Ireland, 1973-1974.

'They think they have pacified Ireland. They think that they have purchased half of us and intimidated the other half. They think they have foreseen everything, think that they provided against everything; but the fools, the fools, the fools! – they have left us our Fenian dead, and while Ireland holds these graves, Ireland unfree shall never be at peace.'

— *Padraig Pearse, Irish Nationalist leader, at the funeral of Jeremiah O'Donovan Rossa, 1915.*

1916

The Easter Rising

On Easter Monday 1916 about 1,400 armed men (Irish Volunteers, IRB and Citizen Army) under the command of Padraig Pearse, polished off the last of their Easter eggs and then took control of about ten key buildings around the centre of Dublin. Pearse himself seized the GPO in O'Connell Street and after sending a postcard to his Mammy to let her know he'd arrived safely, emerged to read aloud the Proclamation of the Irish Republic. It was signed by Thomas J Clarke, Seán Mac Diarmada, Thomas MacDonagh, Éamonn Ceannt, P H Pearse, James Connolly and Joseph Plunkett. This was greeted with bemusement and anger by most Dubliners, especially any unfortunate eejit who'd just popped in to buy a stamp. The proclamation declared Ireland to be a Sovereign Independent State, guaranteed liberty and equal rights for everyone and generally told the British that they were as welcome in Ireland as

a fart in an elevator. While this was going on, other groups of Volunteers were seizing the Four Courts, a former workhouse called the South Dublin Union (now St James's Hospital), St Stephen's Green, Boland's Bakery and Jacob's Biscuit Factory, so at least they'd have plenty

WHAT TIME IS THE RISING OVER AT? I TOLD THE MOT I'D BE HOME FOR 6.

to eat and they might at last solve the mystery of how they got the figs into the Fig Rolls. A small group occupied a house overlooking Mount Street Bridge and this position would see the single biggest number of fatalities. With law and order temporarily abandoned, the poorer Dublin citizenry imagined they could see giant 'All Stocks Must Go!' signs in the shop windows and they began helping themselves to everything they could lay their hands on. No doubt it never crossed their minds as they looted Clery's (directly opposite the GPO) that it was owned by the guy who'd organised the lockout three years earlier and starved them into submission. Meanwhile, the rebels cocked their rifles and waited.

Sir Roger Casement

An Irishman, but a British consul, Casement spent much of his life abroad, exposing first the brutality of the Belgian King Leopold II in the Congo and then turning his attention to the murderous abuse by the Peruvian Amazon Rubber Company against the Putumayo Indians, for which he was awarded a knighthood. This was ironic really, as it was these experiences that opened his eyes to British abuses of power in Ireland! He was executed for treason in 1916 after trying to smuggle arms from Germany. Afterwards British Intelligence released what they claimed were his diaries, detailing criminal promiscuous homosexual activity. Experts still cannot agree whether these were genuine or forged to discredit Casement.

1916

The British Response
Bloody Paddys!

The initial British response to the Rising was to send a small force of Lancers trotting up the middle of O'Connell Street for a jolly old gander at the bit of a tiff in the Post Office, don't you know! The insurgents opened fire and four of the unfortunate lancers fell dead. Suddenly the British were planking it as the scale of the problem dawned on them – and they only had 1,200 men in the city. They called for reinforcements and the gunboat 'The Helga' sailed up the Liffey where it proceeded to flatten Liberty Hall with shell fire, British 'Intelligence' having failed to let them know that this building was completely empty. Determined to demonstrate their imcompetence to the full, the Helga's guns continued to fire into the city, sometimes with such inaccuracy or lack of concern for the lives of civilians that their own men thought they were being attacked by rebel gunfire and they started shooting at each other! They also nearly destroyed the Viceregal Lodge in the Phoenix Park (three miles away!). After a lot of practice shots, (200 buildings destroyed), the guy working the guns finally found his glasses and proceeded to rain shells down on the GPO.

JAYSUS, I ONLY WENT IN TO GET A BLEEDIN' STAMP.

1916

Reinforcements Arrive

As the GPO was slowly shelled into submission, the arrival of about 17,000 British reinforcements sort of tipped the odds in their favour. The heaviest fighting took place near Mount Street Bridge across the Grand Canal where a group of fifteen rebels inflicted 240 casualties on the British – reportedly their commander repeatedly ordered his raw recruits to try to take the bridge with a headlong charge – headlong into a hail of bullets. He continued this tactic despite the fact that bodies were piled high on the bridge – makes you wonder how these guys ever built an empire? But as the week wore on, the greater numbers and heavier firepower began to turn the tide of the Rising.

INTERESTING STUFF

The Amazing Countess Markievicz

Born Constance Gore-Booth, daughter of a wealthy (but humanitarian) Anglo-Irish landlord, married to a Polish Count, she was the first woman MP in the House of Commons, first woman in Europe to hold a cabinet position, militant suffragette, champion of the poor (sold virtually all her possessions to feed Dublin's starving), a landscape painter and literary intellectual, friend of WB Yeats who immortalised her in poetry. She was an officer in the 1916 Rising, arrested and sentenced to death (commuted 'on account of her sex'), fought on the Republican side in the Civil War, jailed again, elected to Dâil (4th time) in 1927, died aged fifty-nine before she could take her seat. And career women today talk about multi-tasking!

Constance Markievicz still keeping an eye over proceedings in St Stephen's Green

Surrender

On Saturday, 29 April, just five days after it had started, the Rising ended. Pearse & Co had been forced to abandon the GPO due to the fact that it was mostly a pile of concrete. Having retreated to a fish shop in Moore Street, the prospect of civilian deaths, not to mention the smell of rotten mackerel, hastened their decision. Pearse signed the document of surrender under the eyes of the British commander, General Maxwell, already licking his lips at the prospect of commanding so many firing squads. Soon afterwards all rebel positions laid down their arms. The last to do so were those at Boland's Mill under Eamon de Valera. After an overnight stay in the

gardens of the Rotunda, the remaining rebels were marched down Sackville Street (O'Connell Street) mostly to the jeers of Dubliners, many of whom threw fruit at the rebels with more accuracy than the British shelling.

CAPTAIN, I'VE BEEN HIT.

1916

Che Aftermath of the Rising

Over the next couple of weeks, General Maxwell had 3,500 people arrested, held hundreds of 'trials' where there was no jury and no defence and sentenced ninety people to death. Fifteen were executed, including Pearse and all the other signatories of the Proclamation. Connolly was too ill to stand but why let that get in the way of a good execution? He was strapped to a chair, carried out to the yard in Kilmainham Gaol and shot. De Valera escaped death because he'd been born in America and the British wanted desperately to suck up to the Americans so they'd come over and save their arses in WW1.

IF WE'RE TO BELIEVE LATER CLAIMS, THE VOLUNTEERS IN THE GPO NUMBERED HUNDREDS OF THOUSANDS

Maxwell was on a roll, but suddenly the British government realised that there was a wave of revulsion at their actions, Not just in Ireland but in Europe and the US. Oh shit, they'd done it again – created a whole new generation of martyrs. When many of the surviving rebels were marched through Dublin, crowds six deep cheered them and gave them a hero's send-off. The executed leaders were only in their graves a few days and already their ghosts had come back to haunt the British.

Inside the GPO, 1916

INTERESTING STUFF

Till death us do part.

One of the leaders of the Rising, poet Joseph Mary Plunkett, married his sweetheart, Grace Gifford, in the tiny chapel of Kilmainham Gaol shortly before his execution. They had been due to marry on Easter Sunday, but that had proved difficult, as about then Joe was polishing his rifle in preparation for some shooting practice from the GPO. The wedding was witnessed by soldiers who stood around with bayonets fixed. Joseph and Grace were separated immediately after the ceremony. A few hours later, he was dead. Grace never re-married.

The Rise of Sinn Féin

Tiocfaidh Armani

Up until now Sinn Féin was basically a loose collection of Irish-speaking ideological nationalists who used to meet at weekends, sing a few rebel songs, have a pint and never really do anything. Arthur Griffith, its founder, was still leader. Eamon de Valera was released from prison in England in 1917 and no sooner was he off the boat than he'd won a seat in the House of Commons, defeating a Home Rule candidate. This was a reflection of the mood in the country – in fact the country was still in a really lousy mood with the British after the Rising. Most of those arrested had been banged up in Frongoch Prison camp in Wales. This became known as Sinn Féin University as it was the primary seat of learning of new ways to throw the Brits out of Ireland. Among the inmates was Michael Collins, who, while

GRADUATE OF THE
SINN FÉ IN UNIVERSITY 1917

there, performed the admirable feat of winning a 100 yard race in 10.8 seconds. Other events that day were the 'Hit the guard with a piece of shite from 25 metres' and the '50-yard tunnel digging sprint'. When these men returned under amnesty in 1917 there was a vast supply of young, energetic, pissed-off Republicans ready to do their bit. In October that year De Valera ousted Arthur Griffith as leader of Sinn Féin.

1918 – 19

The Declaration of Independence

There was a general election in Ireland and Britain the following year and Sinn Féin's main bene-factors in this were the British. Not that they provided campaign funds or anything. No, they began conscripting soldiers in Ireland. There was vast opposition from all parties, from the Church and from the labour movement, who organised a general strike. As a result, by the time WW1 had ended the British had managed to conscript roughly two one-legged pensioners, a mongrel with fleas and a dray horse called Biddy. Also as a result Sinn Féin won almost three quarters of the seats in the election. Just a few weeks later, the victorious Sinn Féin convened the first Dáil in the Round Room of the Mansion House. Ireland was declared a sovereign state, given the name The Irish Republic, and The Declaration of Independence was read.

'He comes from a brainy Cork Family.'

—————— *First line of a British police dossier on Michael Collins,*
Irish Nationalist Leader, discovered by Collins himself
during a raid on Dublin Castle

1919 – 1921

The War of Independence

The new Irish Republic needed an army, and the original Irish Volunteers would do just nicely – except they were now named the Irish Republican Army. These are often referred to as the 'old' IRA, not because they were a bunch of doddery oul' farts, but to distinguish them from the present-day IRA. Coinciding with the day of the first Dáil, a group of republicans attacked and killed two constables who were escorting explosives. The first shots had been fired in the war of Independence. This would set the pattern for the next two years: the IRA, mainly under the direction of Michael Collins, engaged in a guerilla-style war against the largely Catholic Royal Irish Constabulary. They ambushed and killed policemen, burnt out rural police stations and stole their weapons, shot magistrates who they considered unjust, intimidated RIC men into leaving the force and boycotted the police and their families so that often the only way they could buy their food was by pointing a gun at the grocer's head. The grocers rarely gave them their loyalty points.

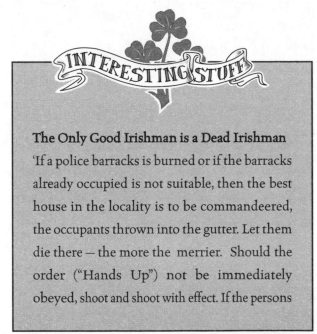

INTERESTING STUFF

The Only Good Irishman is a Dead Irishman
'If a police barracks is burned or if the barracks already occupied is not suitable, then the best house in the locality is to be commandeered, the occupants thrown into the gutter. Let them die there — the more the merrier. Should the order ("Hands Up") not be immediately obeyed, shoot and shoot with effect. If the persons

approaching (a patrol) carry their hands in their pockets, or are in any way suspicious-looking, shoot them down. You may make mistakes occasionally and innocent persons may be shot, but that cannot be helped, and you are bound to get the right parties some time. The more you shoot, the better I will like you, and I assure you no policeman will get into trouble for shooting any man.' – Lt. Col. Smyth, British Army Officer in a speech to the RIC in June 1920. It may come are a surprise, but Lt Col Smyth was assassinated by the IRA about a month later.

1920

The Black and Tans

The British Government's policy for dealing with the IRA was to officially sanction reprisals – in other words they decided to let the army and RIC have carte blanche to murder whoever they liked, IRA or civilian, it didn't really matter, sure they were only Paddies. But the British could always be relied on to go the extra mile – so they also created a new force officially called the RIC Reserve, but infamously known as the Black & Tans. These were mainly uneducated, unskilled gougers who'd fought in WW1 and were now unemployed, many of them involved in crime. At ten shillings a day and the promise of bashing in some heads, they leapt at the job. In fact so many leapt (7-8,000) that they hadn't enough RIC uniforms to go around, so they gave them a mix of khaki pants and dark green police tunics, hence the name Black & Tans. These boyos were supplemented by another force of ex-officers known as the Auxilliaries, who were reputedly even bigger bastards. When the cages were opened they proceeded to brutalise anyone who looked sideways at them. They sacked cities and towns everywhere, including Cork, Tuam, Trim, Balbriggan, Thurles and Tralee, not to mention countless villages and homes. If the IRA killed an RIC man, they often responded by murdering innocent civil-

LETS TURN THESE PADDIES INTO BLACK AND BLUES!

ians. The irony once again was that every time the Black & Tans shot an IRA man, membership of the IRA rose by about fifty!

INTERESTING STUFF

Ben & Jerry's

To celebrate St Patrick's Day 2006, the US ice cream giant Ben & Jerry's decided to launch a flavour called Black & Tan (based on the drink of that name). Not surprisingly, the ice cream got a very cool reception in Ireland. It seems the company hadn't done their homework and were unaware of the negative connotations 'Black & Tan' had in the oul' sod. A hasty apology was issued to try and melt the frostiness they were sensing from their Irish customers. No ice cream for them that weekend.

1920

Bloody Sunday

Sunday, 21 November 1920 was probably the single most eventful day of the war, as well as the most notorious. It began with Collins ordering the assassination of eighteen British agents who ran a network of spies and informers in Dublin. The eighteen were known as the Cairo gang because a) they frequented The Cairo Coffee House in Grafton Street, b) they'd served in Egypt and c) Collins intended to send them the way of the Pharoes. Collins said he wanted to 'pay them back in their own coin' for atrocities they'd committed. And the IRA didn't short change them, killing fourteen and wounding ten spies before noon. The other coin reference from the day was when the Auxilliaries and RIC reputedly decided to flip a coin to see whether they'd go on a shooting spree in O'Connell Street or Croke Park, where the Dubs were playing Tipperary in a Gaelic football match. Croker won the toss and British forces entered the ground where 10,000 spectators were gathered. Using the excuse that an IRA rebel was hiding in the crowd, they decided their best chance of hitting him was to shoot randomly into the crowd. Fourteen were killed and hundreds injured. The dead included three children, as well as Jeannie Boyle, a girl due to be married the following Friday, and Michael Hogan, a Tipperary player after whom Croke Park's Hogan Stand is named. The massacre made headlines around the world.

1921

The Truce

Surprisingly, it was King George V who made the first moves towards achieving peace. He basically ate the head off Prime Minister Lloyd George for letting the British army and police act like animals, clearly un-aware that this had been official British policy for centuries. Lloyd George was also concerned that the IRA campaign

PEACE MAN

could last for donkey's years and it was costing him a fortune in taxpayer's money – money that could easily be wasted elsewhere, by hiring more civil servants, for example. Unfortunately for the PM, the ironically named 'British Intelligence' weren't aware that the IRA had virtually no weapons or ammunition left. Not surprisingly, when Lloyd George proposed a truce in advance of negotiations, de Valera agreed. The truce came into effect on July 11.

The Treaty
Not so Free State

When negotiations began, de Valera decided not to attend, knowing that if the whole thing turned out arseways he wouldn't be in the firing line, literally. Also, Lloyd George had described negotiating with him as like trying to 'lift mercury with a fork'. Collins himself had referred to 'Dev' as 'The long whore', so it was probably as well he kept away from the negotiating table. The British plan involved Ireland being officially divided in two – six counties in Northern Ireland under their own government and the other twenty-six in the south, to be called the Irish Free State, which would also have its own government but would still be a British dominion – Ireland would still be under the crown. In Dev's eyes that meant under the boot. Lloyd George issued Collins with an ultimatum – a watered down form of independence on one hand or all-out war with Britain on the other. Collins, knowing the IRA's weapons reserve was down to about three slingshots and a packet of stink bombs, reluctantly accepted the deal and signed the Treaty on 6 December 1921. He correcty forecast that it would not play well back home.

FECKIN' QUOTES

'I tell you this – early this morning I signed my death warrant.'

— *Michael Collins, after signing The Treaty*

INTERESTING STUFF

Ernie O'Malley

The character played by Cillian Murphy in 'The Wind that Shakes the Barley' was partly based on O'Malley, which is not surprising, given his colourful life. Studying to be a doctor when the 1916 Rising happened, he was almost persuaded by some Unionist pals to defend Trinity College, but decided 'to hell with that', got a rifle and took a few pot shots at the British. Extremely courageous in battle, he was captured and tortured during the Anglo-Irish war but escaped with the help of a sympathetic British soldier. While fighting for the Anti-Treaty side he was once shot twenty times, captured and only escaped execution when the doctor treating him turned out to be an old buddy from medical school. After the war he travelled in Europe, the US and Mexico, where he mixed with artistic types and wrote a very literary memoir called *On Another Man's Wound.* He became friends with WB Yeats and John Ford and acted as Ford's consultant on the film *The Quiet Man*, starring Maureen O'Hara and John Wayne, for which he has a credit as 'IRA Consultant'! O'Malley was given a state funeral in 1957.

1922

The British Depart
(at last!)

In January, the Dáil ratified the Treaty by sixty-four votes to fifty-seven and Dev immediately resigned as President of the Republic. He and many republicans could no more swear 'to be faithful to His Majesty' than they could eat their own heads. A general election followed and Dev was hoping the people would give him the mandate he needed to tell the Brits where to stick their Treaty. But when the people spoke, he didn't like what they had to say and decided they didn't know their arse from their elbow. Meanwhile, Michael Collins was arriving in Dublin Castle to formally accept the handover from the British. Viceroy FitzAlan remarked to him: 'You are seven minutes late, Mr Collins' to which Collins replied, 'We've been waiting over seven hundred years. You can have the extra seven minutes!'

THE VICEROY WASN'T USED TO BEING KEPT WAITING

The 'Big Fella' in his native Skibbereen

The Civil War

In the early months of 1922 there were many relatively minor clashes between Treaty and anti-Treaty groups but things really started to get hot as summer approached. In April, 200 IRA men began an occupation of the Four Courts building in Dublin. For a couple of months the jury was out on what to do as Collins was determined to avoid all-out civil war but was coming under pressure from Arthur Griffith, now President, and from the British. Sentence was passed in June and Collins began to shell the building, killing many of the insurgents and arresting most of the rest. Unfortunately, one thousand years of public records were also destroyed in the process, which means no

one in Ireland can ever find out who their great-great-great-great granny was. A large group of republicans escaped and retreated to the north end of O'Connell Street into the The Hamman Hotel. They stayed almost a week, by which time many were either dead or had checked out without paying, leaving their rooms in a right state.

The last to die in this action was Cathal Brugha, one of the top anti-Treaty leaders.

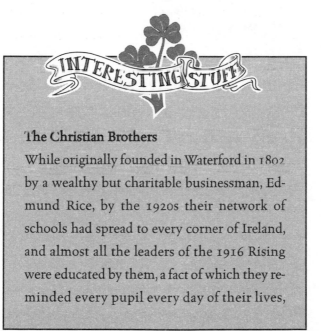

Interesting Stuff

The Christian Brothers

While originally founded in Waterford in 1802 by a wealthy but charitable businessman, Edmund Rice, by the 1920s their network of schools had spread to every corner of Ireland, and almost all the leaders of the 1916 Rising were educated by them, a fact of which they reminded every pupil every day of their lives, with the assistance of a clatter on the back of the head. Their motto is 'Facere et Docere' which means 'Beat the living crap out of them'. However, despite the fact that many CBs were more suited to a career as a bouncer in a docklands bar, many of the Brothers really did do wonders for education in Ireland. In fact, without them, half the country probably wouldn't be able to spell their own name!

The War outside Dublin

The Republic of Cork

With Dublin secured, the attention of Collins's army turned to his own neck of the woods – Munster. Anti-Treaty forces now held Counties Cork, Waterford and Limerick and had proclaimed a 'Munster Republic' with Cork City as its capital. Some of their descendants still regard Cork as the 'real capital' of

Ireland, God love them. Free State forces attacked on two fronts – by land and sea, and the large towns and cities were re-taken relatively easily. The IRA retreated to the countryside where they began a campaign of guerilla warfare – they'd had plenty of practise at this from killing Black and Tans and RIC. A bloody period of attacks and bitter reprisals followed for about

LANGER

CITIZEN OF THE PEOPLES REPUBLIC OF CORK

eight months during which time both sides, but especially the Free State Government, seemed determined to show that they could be just as big a shower of savages as the British. Seventy-seven anti-Treaty rebels were executed during the war and several generations later this has still not been forgotten. The worst atrocity happened at Ballyseedy in County Kerry where nine IRA prisoners were tied to a mine which was then detonated. But, as always seems to happen in these cases, one survived to tell the tale.

The Assassination of Michael Collins

On 12 August 1922 President Arthur Griffith died of a brain haemorrhage. As Collins strode along behind the coffin, he didn't realise that just ten days later he'd be following Griffith to the grave. On a visit to his native Cork, Collins's convoy was ambushed near the village of Béal na mBláth. A gunfight followed and there was one fatality – Collins had been shot in the head. Ironically, it had been rumoured that Collins had been in Cork to try to begin peace talks with the anti-Treaty side. He had his answer. Collins's body lay in state in Dublin for three days and tens of thousand filed past his remains. There were enough conspiracy theories around after his death to rival the assassination of JFK – including it having been the work of a leading anti-Treaty politician or of a British 'plant', but nobody seemed to want to come out and take the 'credit'. Ireland had been robbed of probably the greatest leader it never had – a towering man of intelligence, organisation, bravery and genuine vision. The only similarity most of our subsequent political 'leaders' can claim is that they're tall. And some of them aren't even that. Collins, known simply as 'The Big Fella', was just thirty-one when he died.

LATTER DAY POLITICIANS ALSO HAVE NICKNAMES...

| THE 'ROUND FAT FELLA' | THE 'BIG THICK GOMBEEN FELLA' | THE 'YOU SCRATCH MY BACK FELLA' |

'Here, in Cork district, you have in combination all the dangers which war can inflict.'

Eamon de Valera 1882-1975
Independence fighter, Taoiseach, President of Ireland.

Ceasefire

Because the anti-Treaty forces had little support from the population in general, it was becoming increasingly difficult for them to find a pillow to lay their head upon after a tiring day shooting people. To add to their miseries, they were officially condemned by the Catholic Church who said they would be denied

Confession – in other words the Church had decided that God wouldn't want to forgive them. Consultation with the Almighty doesn't seem to have come into it! This further distanced the rebels from the ordinary

people. IRA arms were also in short supply, but Liam Lynch, one of their leaders, seemed determined to fight until his last breath, which wasn't far away. Dev, meanwhile, who had taken no part in the fighting, called for a ceasefire, but it was only after Lynch was killed in the Knockmealdown mountains in Tipperary that the new leadership agreed to lay down arms in May 1923.

1922 and beyond

The Legacy of the Civil War

Besides the loss of lives (3-4,000), the estimated cost (£40-£50 million), and the loss of or damage to so many fine buildings, there was also the loss of innocence – up until then Ireland had been under the often tyrannical rule of a superpower. Now we'd learned that, given half a chance, we could be just as big a bunch of bastards to each other. And, for generations to come, the two sides hated and distrusted each other, cheerily passing their simmering resentment down to their children, in song, story and verse, before they were out of nappies. Ireland's two largest parties, Fianna Fáil and Fine Gael, are also direct descendants of the parties that existed then. Despite the fact that policy-wise they are virtually identical, to this day the poor sods can't unshackle themselves from their past. Both lots would happily get into bed with parties that are far to their left or right before they'd be prepared to breathe the same air as their civil war rivals (four generations removed). God forbid they should ever put the greater good of Ireland first.

SPOT THE DIFFERENCE

'Irish Alzheimer's: you forget
everything except the grudges.'

——— Judy Collins, American Folk Singer/Songwriter, b 1939

1926

The Founding of Fianna Fáil

We're on the one road

🍇 In 1926, Dev decided to give actual politics a try as a means of achieving his goals and duly formed Fianna Fáil, who a few years later would win a majority in the general election and stay in Government for the next 16 years. In fact, Fianna Fáil would remain in power (with a rare stint in opposition) for pretty much all of eternity and beyond. Whatever magic Dev had worked, it seems his party could do no wrong in the eyes of the people, something that is patently a load of 'oul bollox. In fact, Dev himself would stay as leader of the party until 1959 and then become president until 1973. He retired aged 90, at the time the oldest head of state in the world and died in 1975. Some of his colleagues decided to honour his memory by making Fianna Fáil synonymous with words like 'cute hoor', 'GUBU' 'gombeen man' and 'brown envelope'.

INTERESTING STUFF

Women's Suffrage in Ireland

The 1916 Proclamation is one of the first such documents to specifically recognize the equality of both 'Irishmen and Irishwomen' (The US Declaration of Independence, for example, recognizes 'all men are created equal'.) Indeed one of the Rising's leaders was a woman greatly admired by both sexes, Countess Markievicz (see page 184) She was also one of the top suffragists of her day. Another famous nationalist and suffragist couple of the time were Francis Skeffington and Hanna Sheehy. To make his

point, Francis took the then unheard of decision to adopt his wife's name when they
married, making him Francis Sheehy-Skeffing-
ton. Despite all their efforts, it would be 1928
before women actually got the vote in Ireland.

DEMOCRACY FOREVER
TEASES US WITH THE
CONTRAST BETWEEN
IDEALS AND REALITIES

WOW! REALLY
IMPRESSIVE!!!

1932

The Blueshirts

As a response to members of the IRA disrupt-
ing meetings of Cumann na nGaedhael (the forerunner of Fine Gael) and kicking the crap out of its
members, Eoin O'Duffy, a former leader of the IRA and
a pro-Treaty politician, founded a fascist group 'to defend democracy'. This was modelled on Germany's

Brownshirts and Italy's Blackshirts. Originally called the Pink and White Polka-Dotshirts, the group were re-named the Blueshirts because nobody would take them seriously. The same Eoin O'Duffy would found Fine Gael in 1933, and the party would contest many general elections against Fianna Fáil over the next seventy years ... well, contest in the same way Cobh Ramblers would contest a match with Real Madrid. In August 1933, O'Duffy planned a 'March on Dublin' to commemorate the likes of Michael Collins and Arthur Griffith. Dev banned the march, basically because he was worried O'Duffy might fancy himself as a little Hitler and stage a coup! Luckily, O'Duffy cancelled the march and Ireland's brief brush with fascism was as short- lived as a Government election manifesto promise.

'Beware of the man whose God is in the skies.'

George Bernard Shaw, Irish Playwright, 1856-1950

De Valera's Constitution

Comely Maidens and All That

Dev didn't like the existing Constitution. Firstly, it had been drafted by pro-Treaty politicians who he regarded as slightly above intestinal parasites on the evolutionary chain. Secondly, while he'd already gotten rid of references to 'Oaths of Allegiance to the King' and the 'British Crown', he really wanted a clean slate so he could introduce a load of his own old bollox to replace the British crap. When Edward VIII abdicated from the throne so he could go gallivanting with Mrs Simpson, the poor Brits were left chasing their tails. And considering that they'd always had their head up their arse regarding Ireland anyway, it gave Dev the perfect opportunity to put his constitution to the people, who duly gave it their endorsement, but not by much. In most regards the 1937 Constitution was

I THINK THE LORD LEFT THE TAP RUNNING

grand, guaranteeing freedom, equality before law, right to education etc etc. The problem was that it gave the Catholic Church a 'special position' in the state. The bishops and priests took this to mean 'absolute power' and set about screwing up the country sexually for generations and denying everyone basic rights like access to contraception, divorce and Playboy Magazine. For Christ's sake, the guy who Dev had approve the Constitution – Archbishop John Charles McQuaid – was such a nutter he actually banned tampons because he thought they might get women excited! Ah, God be with the innocent days.

Operation Emerald

Falling back on the tried and trusted mantra, 'England's enemy is our bosom buddy', in the early stages of WWII the IRA actually tried to establish some ties with Germany, hoping to secure arms. This never really panned out but old Adolf did in fact have a contingency plan to invade Ireland, called 'Operation Emerald', the theory being to sneak around the back and give Britain a kick up the arse. Though never averse to kicking Britain anywhere, most Irish people will have been pleased this never happened, as they didn't fancy being pestered by another foreign power for another feckin' seven hundred years. Incidentally, maybe Adolf's interest in Ireland came from the fact that his sister-in-law was a Dub called Bridget Dowling!

MEIN GOTT IN FECKIN' HIM-MEL

World War II

🍀 The good news is that this never actually happened. Whereas every other country in the world experienced 'World War II', Ireland got 'The Emergency'. Dev had decided to keep Ireland out of the war, or rather, it would simply have stuck in the country's craw to have supported Britain during the war. After all, we'd only just gotten rid of them. This pissed
them off no end, which was grand with most Irish people who still had memories of their presence. Having said that, more than 75,000 Irish men did actually go and serve with the Allies during the war, and Irish Intelligence did actually pass on information to Britain, and Irish firefighters did help their Belfast comrades put out fires, and Ireland did provide crucial weather information on D-Day, so we weren't completely, absolutely, 100% neutral. Apart from the rationing,

WAR?
WHAT
WAR?

our worst experience of the war was when the Germans bombed northside Dublin, killing thirty-eight people. They said it was a mistake but many believed it was a warning not to join the Allies. If they'd known Dev's views on the Brits, they could have saved their bombs. And if proof of this was needed, Dev provided it when Adolf blew his brains out and Dev formally – and eerily - offered his condolences to the German people. After the war, Churchill came on the radio and moaned about how Ireland hadn't supported the British and that Britain had 'stood alone'. Dev redeemed himself somewhat in Irish people's eyes by pointing out that Ireland had stood alone not for a couple of years but through 700 years of tyranny. So shove that in your feckin' cigar and smoke it, Winston.

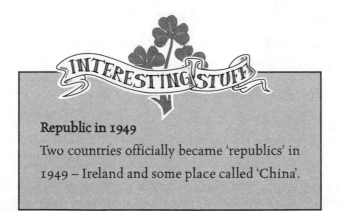

Republic in 1949

Two countries officially became 'republics' in 1949 – Ireland and some place called 'China'.

> Luckily, we didn't have the subsequent 'cultural revolution' which saw huge purges of politicians in China. Instead we had the 'cute hoors' revolution which would see the beginning of the tradition of politicians and rich businessmen scratching each others backs for generations to come.

1945 – 1970

Ireland after 'The Emergency'

Ireland's economic policies of the late Forties and Fifties were as effective as a lifebelt made of lead. High tariffs kept manufacturing costs so high that the only thing we could shift abroad were half the bleedin' population. De Valera's vision of a rural idyll with 'comely maidens dancing at the crossroads' and a people 'given to frugal living' was beginning to seem short-sighted, and indeed Dev was literally becoming short-sighted himself. It was only in 1959 when Sean

Lemass became Taoiseach and reversed many of Dev's policies, completely opening up the economy, that Ireland began to catch up with the rest of Europe in terms of modernization, industrialization and even in social terms. Fianna Fáil's Lemass is regarded by many (of all political shades) as 'the architect of modern Ireland' and one of the most visionary leaders Ireland has ever had. His legacy probably accounts for much of the popularity that Fianna Fáil continues to enjoy today, especially as it's difficult to find anything else that accounts for it.

INTERESTING STUFF

Ireland joins the EEC

The EEC, for those younger readers, was the European Economic Community, which was the forerunner of the EC or the European Community, which was the forerunner of the EU, the European Union, which will probably be the forerunner of the USE or the United States of Europe. We joined it in 1973 and have been enthusiastic members ever since for two reasons - a) the British aren't that keen on Europe so anything that distances us from them is considered good, and b) over the last few decades the Europeans have given us literally tons of free money.

COOL! FREE FRANCS AND DEUTSCHMARKS

Northern Ireland after the War

The partition agreed in the 1921 Treaty had created six counties north of the border which had a large Protestant majority. This was grand with their Prime Minister James Craig, who pretty much nailed his colours to the mast when he'd said he wanted a 'Protestant parliament in a Protestant state'. Many of his successors and their cronies would gladly have nailed a few Catholics to the mast as well as they regarded them as a bunch of lowlife Taigs and were paranoid about being dragged into a united Ireland. This wasn't without foundation as the Republic's constitution held a territorial claim over the six counties. Craig's original declaration had been in response to Dev's statement that Ireland would be a 'Catholic nation'. Of course the difference in the south was that the minority Protestant community had loads of dosh and influence and suffered little or no discrimination. In the post-war north, local councils were almost exclusively Protestant-controlled and even in areas like Derry, where there was a higher proportion of Catholics, gerrymandering maintained things just the way the bigots liked it – Catholic-free. Catholics were housed in estates not fit for dogs, could only get the crappiest jobs and generally had to endure institution-alised discrimination. The Royal Ulster Constabulary was overwhelmingly Protestant and frequently used their truncheons to hammer home this point to Catholics. The lesson of Irish history was that you could only pile up so much injustice behind a dam be-fore it burst. Sadly, the Protestant leaders hadn't been paying attention in class that day. And of course, in 1968, the dam burst.

'One American said that the most interesting thing about Holy Ireland was that its people hate each other in the name of Jesus Christ. And they do!'

———— Bernadette Devlin, Socialist Republican Politician, b 1947

The Troubles

When a group of Catholic civil rights activists tried to stage a peaceful protest march in Derry in October 1968, the RUC baton charged them and basically battered the crap out of them – all beautifully captured on TV camera for the world to see. The IRA, who'd been pretty much a spent force then and had little or no connection with the freedom fighters of the Twenties, now used this event and the subsequent introduction of internment (imprisonment without trial) as a recruiting tool. The British and Unionists may as well have stuck up a sign reading 'Anti-British Terrorists wanted urgently.' Downtrodden, bitter and frustrated young men and women signed up in their droves. The British government soon sent in the army, initially to protect the Catholics against their Protestant neighbours, and they were initially welcomed. Well, for about fifteen minutes anyway. And now that the world was watching, the British suddenly decided that allowing a government that was part of their 'great nation' – not 300 miles from London – to practise blatant discrimination against a large minority wasn't terribly good PR. So they introduced direct rule. There then followed thirty years of IRA terrorism, state-sponsored murder, brutality, fanaticism, internment without trial, intransigence, injustice, hunger strikes, wrongful arrests, the murder of innocents by all sides, collusion between terrorists and government, punishment shootings, rioting, destruction of homes and property, intimidation and hatred. 3523 dead.

Not a place to go for your holliers in dem days.

The Swinging Sixties

Well, they didn't exactly swing in Ireland as have a bit of a hop and skip. Attitudes were changing to social issues in Ireland, but at a snail's pace compared to Europe. The Catholic Church's grip on the nation's morals was as tight as ever, even though their own morals at the time needed a good squeeze, as the future would reveal. Anyway it wasn't all bad. We had the showband era when as many as 800 bands were playing to screaming hordes of youngwans and youngfellas all across the country. RTE launched its television service in 1961 and kept the same bunch of presenters for the next 40 years. Dunnes Stores introduced Ireland to the concept of the 'Supermarket' with the opening of its store in Cornelscourt – nowadays there are two supermarkets for every person in the country. Croker broke attendance records for Down v Offaly – 90, 556! Down won. JFK came on a state visit and was assassinated back in Texas a month later. And on the 50th anniversary of the 1916

Rising, the IRA thought it would be fun to evict the last remaining Englishman from O'Connell Street – Lord Nelson. They blew his towering pillar to pieces, leaving visitors to Dublin no high viewing point from which to admire the city's architecture – the lucky bastards!

Monuments to Dublin Humour

Irish people have always had a sense of humour and nowhere is this more evident than in the healthily disrespectful nicknames Dubliners have given to their various monuments. A notoriously ugly fountain (The Anna Livia) representing the River Liffey once sat in the middle of O'Connell Street. It featured a reclining 'woman' in a rush of water. This was renamed 'The Floozy in the Jacuzzi'. Its replacement, the Dublin Spire, is known as The Erection at the Intersection, among other things. James Joyce, complete with cane, is called 'The Prick with the Stick' and a bronze of two lady shoppers is 'The Hags with the Bags'. The statue of Oscar Wilde in Merrion Square is called 'The Quare in the Square' and, of course, everyone's favourite, the busty and buxom statue of Molly Malone with her cart near Grafton Street – 'The Tart with the Cart'!

Molly Malone with her
'cockles and mussels'

The Glam Seventies

The increasing access to television and radio from abroad was beginning to tell in everyday conversations, which had undergone subtle changes from comments like 'Yes Michael, she's a fine, upstanding Catholic girl' to 'Jaysus Mick, lookit de arse on yer one!' Films introduced us to attitudes and images we'd never seen before, although the images were usually cut short just when they got to the good bits by an ever-strict censorship. In 1970 we began down a road of conquest that would see us dominate the world – not in soccer, rugby or athletics, but in Eurovision wins! Dana's trailblazing victory (six more to come) would forever give us a reputation as the fountain of naff, empty-headed ditties more suitable to a washing powder jingle. We also joined the EEC (that's the EU to you) because they were giving away free money and the economy was just starting to go down the tubes. Decimal currency arrived, giving Ireland's shopkeepers their first opportunity to rip off all their customers en masse, thereby beginning a tradition that would endure to the present. Ireland's second TV channel, 'Network 2' was launched, presenting us with the opportunity to see twice the amount of crap, and a year later we got our second radio station, 2FM, its name conveniently ignoring the fact that there were about 150 pirate stations in operation. Pope John Paul II visited Ireland and said mass to 1,000, 000 people in the Phoenix Park - there was an awful crush at the gates when 100,000 of them tried to leave after communion. And last but not least, Charles Haughey began his first of three terms as Taoiseach in 1979. Gluttons for punishment, us Paddies.

The Atrocious Eighties

Well, only in economic terms. There were good bits, but it's hard to see through the fog of economic despair as we spiralled down the plughole of bankruptcy, both monetarily and ethically. In the early Eighties, there seemed to a new government every time Kerry won an all Ireland (they won their fourth in a row in 1981 before Offaly famously stopped them in the last minute). One minute it was Fianna Fáil, the next some brutal Fine Gael-Labour coalition, then Charlie again with the help of Tony Gregory and the famous 'Gregory Deal' and then Fine Gael-Labour again under Garret FitzGerald – and it wasn't even 1983 yet! The problem was, none of them had a clue how to get us out of the economic doldrums. Charlie told us to tighten our belts while he was having to put extra holes in his own. Garret was putting taxes on kids' shoes and upsetting every Joe Soap in the street. About a quarter of the population had no work and were legging it abroad. There were strikes every other week, and to add to the gloom, in the mid 80s we had three of the wettest summers on record! But never mind. We did demonstrate our incredibly deep pockets, despite our poverty, when we collectively donated £3m to Bob Geldof's Third World fundraiser, Live Aid. Bob, one of our own, would later be knighted by the Queen for his efforts. We also had the launch of The National Lottery in 1987, giving us all hope that we could become millionaires overnight. Others described it as a 'tax on lunacy'. And in 1987 we had what was, until then, arguably our single greatest international sporting achievement when Stephen Roche won the Tour de France and got to share his momentous moment on the podium with our good old Taoiseach. On yer bike, Charlie!

FECKIN' QUOTES

'He was a one-off, a unique figure of medieval power, intrigue and complexity, surrounded by mystery and money, and protected by populism and cleverness and the well-timed one-liner.'

———— *Maire Geoghegan-Quinn, speaking of three-time Irish Prime Minister Charles Haughey, who died June 13, 2006*

The Booming Nineties

🍇 By the end of the Eighties, successive governments, unions, industries and countless self-interest
groups had made such a financial hames of the country
that we were staring into oblivion. They all then suddenly
discovered the one magic formula that could save us
– co-operation. Well it was that or bust, literally. Social
partnership became the new buzz-word and taxes
were cut to encourage job growth, foreign investment
and more opportunities to go to the pub and get gee-
eyed. And to help get us in more optimistic mood, the
decade also got off to a great start when Ireland qual-
ified for Italia '90 under the stewardship of an Englishman – Jack Charlton. We somehow managed to make
it all the way to the quarter-finals without winning a single match and having scored only 2 goals in 5 games!
1990 also saw Mary Robinson elected as Ireland's first
female President – the victory for Mná na hÉireann another sign that we were beginning to break the social
shackles of the past, and Jaysus we had a lot of
shackles. In 1992 we entered totally unchartered water

when Bishop Eamon Casey resigned after admitting fathering a child, this after lecturing us to bleedin' death for decades about the evils of pre-marital sex! In an instant it seemed that the Catholic Church's reputation as keeper of the nation's morals collapsed and

suddenly everyone was desperate to make up for all the illicit sex they'd missed out on all those years. By the end of the decade many of the previously absolute mortal sins had been embraced, including divorce, contraception and homosexuality. In fact, the Nineties saw nine referenda on various issues. Charlie Haughey finally took his leave of politics in 1992 and we would learn later of his love for Charvet shirts purchased at taxpayer's expense while many of us would have given the shirt off our back for a job. His replacement as Taoiseach, Albert Reynolds, would in 1994 suffer the embarrassment of waiting interminably to greet the Russian President Boris Yeltsin at Shannon Airport, un-aware that Boris was totally bollixed drunk inside the plane. One of the great tragedies of the decade was the murder of journal-ist Veronica Geurin in 1996. This led to a Government crackdown on organised crime, 'too little too late' seeming to be the modus operandi of all governments in our fair land. Ireland got two new TV stations in the Nineties – TG4 and TV3, one of which most people couldn't watch because they had-n't a clue what was being said, and the other they couldn't watch because the imported programmes they showed were so shite. Gay Byrne left the 'Late

KEEP CIRCLING UNTIL I'VE FINISHED THE VODKA

BORIS, YOU FINISHED THE VODKA AN HOUR AGO. THAT'S THE AIRLINE COOLANT

Late Show' in 1999 after thirty-seven years of broach-
ing taboo subjects. Unlike former Taoiseach Jack
Lynch who'd famously decided to put the issue of con-
doms 'on the long finger', good old Gaybo demon-
strated their use by actually putting one on his long
finger! And of course we got our own teflon Taoiseach
in the shape of Bertie Ahern, and while nothing else
stuck, Bertie himself was to stick around for a decade.
We would later discover his regular trips over to Manchester in the 90s were to indulge in the excessive
wealth of, eh, talent of the Manchester United team,
of course. But never mind all that, it's December '99
and we all have to leg it to the off-licence to buy some
booze for the party of the millennium ...

Peace in
Northern Ireland
All Over Bar the Shouting

You could draw up a list the length of your arm
(in fact both arms, your legs and all other bodily ap-
pendages put together) of politicians who claim to be
the one who ended the troubles in Northern Ireland.

Gougers from both sides of the conflict stand grinning for the cameras in the hope they'll be immortalised as The Great Peacemaker. The reality is that the man most responsible for the beginning of the end was John Hume, leader of the nationalist SDLP Party in Northern Ireland, who in the late 1980s did the unthinkable – he began talks with a terrorist organisation, the IRA. By Jaysus, was he slated by politicians on all

SO WE'RE ALL AGREED, THE PUBS SHOULD DEFINITELY BE ALLOWED TO OPEN ON GOOD FRIDAY!

THE FIRST GOOD FRIDAY AGREEMENT

sides and by the media. In fact, he was slated openly by many of the gombeen men you can now see grinning for the cameras and taking the plaudits. As a result of these talks the IRA called a ceasefire in 1994, (broke it in '96 and resumed it in '97). A year later came the famous Good Friday Agreement between the

Unionists, Sinn Féin, the Irish and British Governments. Naturally, even after the agreement had been reached, it took the lot of them almost a decade before they could actually agree on anything. When they did, Northern Ireland finally got its own parliament and Ireland has been treated to the mind-boggling sight of the hardline Unionist Ian Paisley (subsequently First Minister, now retired) sitting chuckling with the man he previously branded a terrorist, the equally hardline Martin McGuinness of Sinn Féin (Deputy First Minister.) The only place Irish people had previously seen anything remotely like this had been back in the Sixties after taking a dose of LSD. Ah, it's good to talk.

'Making peace, I have found, is much harder than making war.'

Gerry Adams, President of Sinn Féin b 1948

The Celtic Tiger

It would be easy to be cynical about the so-called 'Celtic Tiger' economic boom of the last decade or so, so let's be cynical then. One day we're bordering on bankruptcy, then overnight it seemed, it became so easy to get a job any gobshite as thick as a heifer's arse could become a government minister. We had a huge influx of immigrants from eastern Europe, the main effect of which was to make us realise how bleedin' ugly we all are. Bank managers who had previously been as tight as a camel's arse in a sandstorm would now lend you limitless amounts of money to squander on huge, petrol-guzzling 4-wheel drives that you desperately needed to drive to the hairdressers or the newsagents. The price of property went through the roof, making estate agents extremely rich for doing very little and parties mind-numbingly dull as everyone had their tits bored off by someone spouting about how much their shoebox apartment was worth. For the government, the Celtic Tiger was a wonderful opportunity to haul in the cash and then squander it on projects that cost three times their estimate and took twice as long to complete. Naturally, everyone with a product or service to supply saw it as the opportunity of a lifetime to rip-off their fellow countryfolk and our visitors alike. On the upside, it was wonderful not to have to watch another generation wasted on the scrapheap of unemployment and poverty. Almost everyone had access to basic health services (so long as you were prepared to go on a waiting list for anything from 6 months to 3 years), most of us had warm homes, access to education for our chislers and plenty of food on the table, even if most of it was

THE COLLAPSE OF THE CELTIC TIGER

stuff you cook in the microwave for two minutes. The problem was that we went from so low to so high in such a short time it left our heads spinning – much of the spinning the result of a huge increase in alcohol consumption, as everyone sat there getting gee-eyed trying to figure out how to spend all the loot their bank manager had been so kind to lend them. And the fact that more and more people were snorting cocaine was as plain as the nose on their face. We'd actually lost the run of ourselves so much that all but a handful of people failed to notice that the Celtic Tiger we'd created was about to suddenly turn nasty.

Doom and Gloom

If history has taught us anything, it's that what we sow, we reap. And we'd been sowing the seeds of our own undoing for yonks. Any gobshite knows that if your outgoings exceed your income, it's only a matter of time before you go broke and nasty guys turn up at your gaff and tell you that it's not actually your gaff anymore but the bank's. While for ages we seemed to have an excess of everything we wanted, there appeared to be a complete scarcity of one thing we needed – common sense. People borrowed more than they could afford and the banks were happy to lend them virtually anything they wanted. They also lent builders megabucks to erect countless apartments that would be unsaleable. To make matters worse, the government were giving the builders tax breaks to encourage this practice (hard to credit, isn't it?), despite being warned, almost up to the last minute that the entire edifice was about to come crashing down. Now the banks are in a shambles, the construction industry (which was the only thing propping up the entire she-bang) has collapsed and the only high risers are the unemployment rates. There are enough unsold houses, apartments and offices around the country to accommodate the population of Mexico City. Hopefully, some people were prepared for the inevitable rainy day. Otherwise, if we're to believe the forecasters (and we probably shouldn't), it'll soon be back to patching the knees of our trousers, sending the kids to school with their milk in an old YR sauce bottle and their sambos in a Johnston, Mooney & O'Brien wrapper. There'll be no more of this globe-hoppin' and posh hotels – you'll have to settle for a week freezing your arse off in a caravan in Ballybunion. And half the country will still be living with the Mammy until they're forty. In fact, if you were to believe some of the more pessimistic 'experts', we'll soon be having to grow our own food in the back garden and go foraging in the hedgerows. Which, ironically, is exactly the sort of 'frugal living' that Dev had envisioned for us all those years ago. Ah well, we had almighty craic during the good times, but as they say, it's all history now.

FECKIN' QUOTES

'In Ireland the inevitable never happens and the unexpected constantly occurs.'

Sir John Pentland Mahaffy, Irish classicist and scholar 1839 -1919

For anything else you want to
know about the Irish here's a
sampler from another great
Feckin' book ...

The Feckin' book

of Everything Irish

that'll have ye effin' an' blindin' wojus slang

* blatherin' deadly quotations * beltin' out ballads while scuttered * cookin' an Irish Mammy's recipes * and saying things like 'I *will* in me arse.'

Winner of the
BENJAMIN FRANKLIN AWARD 2007
for Humour

Colin Murphy & Donal O'Dea

welcome to feckin' Ireland

There'll be shenanigans aplenty ahead as we take you on a no-holds-barred, laughter-filled tour of almost every nuance of Irish culture.

Discover how feckin' deadly (not to mention manky) Irish slang can be. Have a gander at some of these words and phrases and you'll soon realize precisely why they're gas craic altogether.

Take a peek under the skirts of sex and love in Ireland through the ages and find out about everything from Ireland's most lustful man to why clingfilm was a vital lovemaking accessory in Ireland in the seventies.

And of course, to really be in tune with what it is to be Irish, you have to know her music. You'll find the words to over twenty-five of the most famous and beloved songs, like "The Banks of My Own Lovely Lee," "Galway Bay," and "The Irish Rover," just to name a few. So the next

time you hear "Danny Boy" being played, you won't have to stand there humming quietly to yourself in the corner…you can now sing along as badly as everyone else!

And finally, to further whet your appetite for learning about the wonders of Irish culture, we've included some of the most famous and delicious Irish recipes ever conceived. There's Dublin Coddle, Boxty, Colcannon, Fruit Brack, Bread Pudding, Black Velvet, and many more. And if any of this food makes you feel as rough as a bear's arse, you can go ahead and bite the back of my bollix.

So, whether you're a fine doorful of a woman or a man so mean you'd steal the sugar out of someone's tea, stop foostering about and get ready to reveal the inner Irish in you. You'd be a right eejit not to!

acting the maggot (expression)

Fooling about in a somewhat boisterous manner.

(usage) "Anto! Will you stop acting de maggot and give the oul' wan back her wheelchair."

always a day late and a pound short (expression)

Extremely unreliable. Prone to promise-breaking.

(usage) The government is always a day late and a pound short.

molly malone
(cockles and mussels)

James Yorkston

The famous ditty about Molly Malone—or as she's known to Dubs since they erected a rather well-endowed statue in her honour—"The Tart with the Cart" or the slightly more complimentary "Dish with the Fish."

In Dublin's fair city where the girls are so pretty
I first set my eyes on sweet Molly Malone,
As she wheeled her wheelbarrow
Through streets broad and narrow,
Crying, "Cockles and mussels, alive, alive–o!"

Chorus:
Alive, alive-o, alive, alive-o,
Crying, "Cockles and mussels, alive, alive–o!"

IRISH COFFEE

My old man used to swear by this unique drink as a remedy for rheumatism. And the more he had of it, the more he swore.

INGREDIENTS
1 measure of Irish whiskey
1 or 2 tsp sugar (demerara, if available)
freshly made hot black coffee
2–4 tsp whipped cream

METHOD
- Warm the Irish whiskey, in a microwave if possible, for 30 seconds.
- Pour whiskey into a warmed 7-ounce Irish Coffee glass and add the sugar.
- Fill with the hot coffee to within half an inch of the top of the glass.
- Stir until the sugar is dissolved.
- Spoon the whipped cream on top of the hot coffee and serve immediately.

THIS COFFEE
IS FECKIN'
MANKY,
GIS ANOTHER
THREE...

ADLY IRISH QUOTATIONS SOME SMART FECKER IN

IRISH SONGS YER OUL' FELLA ALWAYS SANG WHE

SH SEX & LOVE THAT'S NOT FIT FOR DACENT PEOP

ETA MAKE WHEN YOU WERE A LITTLE GURRIER ●

THE BATTER WITH A SHOWER OF SAVAGES ● THE

OW OF THE FIRST ONE ● THE FECKIN' BOOK OF E

JUS SLANG, BLATHERIN' DEADLY QUOTATIONS, BE

MMY'S RECIPES AND SAYING THINGS LIKE 'I WILL

YONE WHO HASN'T BEEN PAYING ATTENTION FOR

E BOOK OF IRISH CHARACTERS ● THE BOOK OF FE

D BOWSIES ● THE BOOK OF DEADLY IRISH QUOTAT

IN' ON ABOUT ● THE BOOK OF IRISH SONGS YER O

Y ● THE FECKIN' BOOK OF IRISH SEX & LOVE THA

VELY IRISH RECIPES YER MA USETA MAKE WHEN Y

YINGS FOR WHEN YOU GO ON THE BATTER WITH A

ANG THAT MAKES A HOLY SHOW OF THE FIRST O

VE YE EFFIN' AN' BLINDIN' WOJUS SLANG, BLATHI

UTTERED, COOKIN' AN IRISH MAMMY'S RECIPES AN

OK OF IRISH HISTORY FOR ANYONE WHO HASN'T

HAT ARE WE FECKIN' LIKE? THE BOOK OF IRISH CH

REAT CRAIC FOR CUTE HOORS AND BOWSIES ● 1

CKER IN THE PUB IS ALWAYS BLATHERIN' ON ABOU

NG WHEN HE WAS JARRED AT A HOOLEY ● THE FE

NT PEOPLE'S EYES ● THE BOOK OF LUVELY IRISH

RRIER ● THE FECKIN' BOOK OF IRISH SAYINGS FOI

ES ● THE 2ND FECKIN' BOOK OF IRISH SLANG THA